nd from reference

ILLUSTRATED GUIDE TO
FLAGS

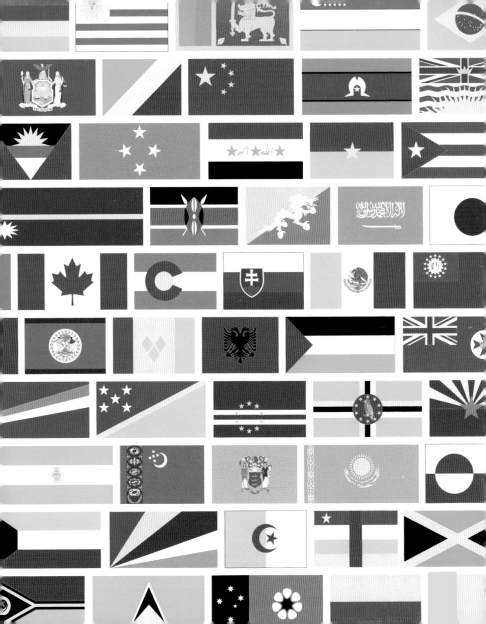

ILLUSTRATED GUIDE TO
FLAGS

JOS POELS

CHARTWELL
BOOKS, INC.

This edition published in 2003 by
CHARTWELL BOOKS, INC.
A division of BOOK SALES, INC
114 Northfield Avenue,
Edison, New Jersey 08837

Produced by
PRC Publishing Ltd, 64 Brewery Road, London N7 9NT

A member of **Chrysalis** Books plc

© 2003 PRC Publishing Ltd.

ISBN 0 7858 1563 5
Printed and bound in Malaysia

The publisher wishes to thank Flag Institute
Enterprises Ltd. for kindly supplying all the images of
flags in this book, including those on the covers.
Maps were supplied by Mountain High Maps® ©
1993 Digital Wisdom, Inc. All other photography was
supplied as follows:
Page 7: © C/B Productions/CORBIS; Page 8: ©
Joseph Sohm; ChromoSohm Inc./CORBIS; Page 11: ©
Dave Bartruff/CORBIS; Pages 15, 23: ©
Hulton|Archive; Page 16: © Bohemian Nomad
Picturemakers/CORBIS; Page 18: © Alan Schein
Photography/CORBIS; Page 19: © Ricki Rosen/COR-
BIS SABA; Page 21: © Archivo Iconografico,
S.A./CORBIS; Page 29: © Richard T. Nowitz/CORBIS;
Page 31: © Bob Krist/CORBIS; Page 34: © Rob
Matheson/CORBIS; Page 37: © Tim Wright/CORBIS;
Page 38: Digital Vision; Page 41: © Owen
Franken/CORBIS; Page 42: © Jonathan Blair/COR-
BIS; Page 47 (top): © Andrew Brookes/CORBIS;
Pages 52, 195: © Karl Weatherly/CORBIS; Page 53: ©
Yogi, Inc./CORBIS; Page 56: © Kevin Fleming/COR-
BIS; Page 91: © Graham Tim/CORBIS SYGMA; Page
103: © Paul A. Souders/CORBIS; Page 127: ©
Richard Berenholtz/CORBIS; Page 167: © Peter
Turnley/CORBIS; Page 233: © Jack Fields/CORBIS.

The author Jos Poels wishes to acknowledge
the invaluable support of Pat Keegan in this
project. Unless otherwise stated in Part 2 the
Gazetteer, all population estimates are correct as
of August 2002.

Contents

Part One

Introduction

POWERFUL SYMBOLS

Flags are one of the oldest forms of communication and have also been used by people as a means of identity. They emphasize who we are, where we come from, what we do, and what our aims are. They are used to communicate without speech, revealing messages through the colors, emblems, and shapes that each have an individual significance. When we look at flags fluttering in the wind, how many of us realize the stories they have to tell us?

Flags have become part of everyday life. They are used by a variety of groups: countries, states, provinces, cities, companies, political parties, clubs, and societies. International organizations also use flags as a means of uniting a group and engendering a sense of belonging.

Primarily used as a means of identification, they can also be used as decoration or as warning signs. They are powerful, communicating across language divides. People could instantly recognize the flag bearer as either friend or enemy, even when they were not able to read or write; the order of the colors and the emblems displayed spoke a universal language that is largely unchanged today.

The importance of flags differs from country to country. In the United States every school day begins with a salute to the Stars and Stripes. People take oaths on their flag, greet it, and will not tolerate it being treated disrespectfully. In some countries the flag is only flown on dates set by law. Design and usage of flags is often regulated by special laws, which stress their importance.

Though recognizable symbols, flags are sometimes seen as just colorful pieces of fabric and the reason for their appearance is frequently forgotten. This book recounts the fascinating histories and the symbolic meaning of the flags of all independent states of the world, as well as the state or provincial flags of the United States of America, Canada, Australia, and the United Kingdom. The stories behind these simple pieces of fabric deal with nearly every aspect of life, bringing the past and future together.

The flags of the world fly outside the Rockefeller Center in New York City, USA.

1 Flags: The Basics

As with nearly every subject, it is necessary to use specialist terms when dealing with flags in order to describe them and explain their usage. These are familiar to a vexillologist—a person who studies all aspects of flags—but may need some explanation for people who have just begun to be interested in flags.

A flag is always described as if the piece of cloth is attached to a flagpole at the left side and is fluttering in the wind. They should be described and "read" from left to right but there are exceptions. When the flag contains Arabic script it is always read from the right to the left.

Every flag has two sides: the front is called the obverse, the back the reverse. The reverse is normally the mirror image of the obverse. Arabic flags with script have two obverse sides, as the script must always be read from right to left. When a flag is charged with a coat of arms that contains words, these words should be fully readable on the reverse as well as the obverse.

The US National and Ohio State flags.

GLOSSARY

Badge: Heraldic emblem, not necessarily a coat of arms. Often used in British ensigns.

Becket: Loop at the end of the hoist rope.

Bicolor: Flag consisting of two colors.

Border: A colored band that surrounds all sides of a flag or a field in a flag. (See also fimbriation)

Canton: The upper-left quarter of a flag. Also recognizable when there is no wind and the flag droops at the flagpole.

Charge: Coat of arms, emblem, or badge placed on the field of the flag.

Countercharged: A charge placed on an invisible line where two colors meet and which reverses them.

Cross: A charge in the form of a vertical cross.

Defaced: An existing flag on which a badge is added.

Ensign: Flag used in ships.

Field: A large single colored central section of the flag.

Fimbriation: A narrow border. (See also border)

Fly: The right two-thirds part of the flag. (See also hoist)

Hoist: The left third part of the flag. (See also fly)

Length: The flag's dimension from left to right. (See also width)

Obverse: The front side of a flag.

Proportions: The ratio of the width to the length of a flag.

Quarterly: A flag or a field divided into four equal sections.

Reverse: The back of a flag.

Saltire: A diagonal cross stretching from corner to corner of the flag.

Serration: Two colors, which are separated by a serrated line.

Swallowtail: A flag, which fly has the shape of a swallowtail. A triangular section is cut out at the fly end.

Triangle: Field in the shape of a triangle, usually to be found at the hoist of a flag.

Tricolour: Flag consisting of three colors, normally three horizontal or vertical bands. (see French national flag, La Tricolore)

Union: Symbol expressing the unification of a country.

Vexilloid: Early form of flag.

Vexillum: A standard.

Width: The flag's dimension along the whole hoist.

FLAG SHAPES

The largest collection of flags can be seen in front of the United Nations building in New York. Every day, the flags of all member states are on display; currently 191 but there are certainly more to come. All of these flags (but one) have one thing in common—they are rectangular. Only the flag of Nepal is different, consisting of two triangular flags which are sewn together.

Today's flags have evolved from a variety of shapes. The earliest predecessor of the current flag shape might be a "gonfanon." This is a long piece of fabric with three or more tails at the fly. It came into use in the ninth century in Europe and was strictly reserved for rulers. Two centuries later, armies also used this shape and later self-governing cities adopted the gonfanon. The current flag of the city of Venice in Italy is still this shape.

Banners in different shapes gradually replaced the gonfanon. Some of these banners were triangular; others were square or were in the shape of a heraldic shield. But the first banners were much deeper than they were wide, so they looked as though a small piece of fabric was stretched along the whole length of the flagpole. Such banners were used by armies and were meant to reinforce who soldiers were to obey in the battlefield.

In the late Middle Ages, ships used square standards for identification purposes. From the 15th and 16th century onward, ships identified themselves by rectangular ensigns. In the beginning they showed a mixture of heraldic devices and designs, as we know them today.

In ships, as well as on the top of castles, a streamer was commonly used. This is a long oblong flag and could measure up to 50 meters. In 1437, the Earl of Warwick had a streamer made that measured roughly eight meters by 40 meters and was charged with the cross of St. George and his personal arms. In 1514, Henry VIII commissioned a streamer for his fleet. It was roughly 50 meters in length, the largest flag ever flown by the British Navy. The use of streamers is still to be found in The Netherlands; when the Dutch show their alliance with their Royal House of Orange, they fly an orange streamer along with their national tricolor flag.

FLAG TYPES

"Flag" is a general term used to describe any piece of flying fabric. There are, however, several types of flags in use. They all have their own function and are used on different and specific occasions.

The best-known flag type is the national flag. This is the type of flag that is in general use by everybody in a particular country. The second part of this book depicts the national flags of all countries of the world.

Some countries also have an alternative national flag called the state flag. The government, its ministries, and its institutions only, use this type of flag. Quite often state flags are charged with the national coat of arms. Germany, for example, has a state flag

that is an unadorned black, red, and yellow triband, charged with the state arms. The flags flown outside the United Nations building in New York are state flags, as they represent the UN members which are governments.

An ensign is a flag used in a ship, normally at the stern, to identify its nationality. Most ensigns are the same as the national flag but some countries have several ensigns. The United Kingdom has the most extended set of ensigns and several commonwealth members (former British dependencies) still follow this British system of ensigns.

A civil ensign is the flag flown in a ship which is part of the merchant navy of a country. The British civil ensign is the red ensign. This consists of a red flag with a

This is the current British civil ensign, used by merchant ships and yachts. It is also used as a courtesy ensign.

miniature version of the Union Flag in the canton.

A government ensign is a special flag used by vessels in government service, but not the Navy. Examples of these are revenue cutters and fishing patrol boats. In the United Kingdom these government ensigns are blue with a small Union Flag in the canton. The national flags of some British dependencies are also of the blue-ensign type, but they are charged with the local badge or arms.

The naval ensign is the special national flag used in navy vessels. They are always much more simply designed than the national or state flag to aid recognition at sea. The British naval ensign is the white ensign: a white flag charged with the St. George Cross and a Union Flag in the canton.

Some countries, such as the United States, have a special yacht ensign. When established in the 19th century, flying this ensign meant the skipper had paid special harbor duties. In the United Kingdom several privileged yacht clubs fly blue or red ensigns defaced by their club badge. These flags may also be used abroad as a replacement of the civil ensign.

The little flag flown at the bow of a naval vessel is called "jack" and, strictly speaking, it is a national flag. Several countries have special jacks, for example, The Netherlands. Though using the national colors, the design is cut up in six triangular pieces and sewn back together in a different order. The nickname of the flag of the United Kingdom is the "Union Jack." This is because in its original form, in 1607, the Union Flag was used as a jack in English and Scottish vessels.

A signal flag is a special flag used to transmit a message. It originated at sea to enable ships to exchange messages by flying their flags in a certain order on their masts. Today there is in existence an international Code of Signals, for transmitting messages with flags. However, these have lost importance due to the development of modern means of communication, such as radio and the Internet.

A state or provincial flag is the flag used by a subdivision of a country. The United

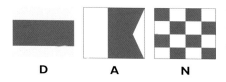
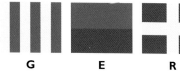

D   **A**   **N**   **G**   **E**   **R**

States consists of states, as does Australia and Brazil. They all have their own state flags. Canada's subdivisions are called provinces, as are those in Belgium and The Netherlands. Russia consists of republics and provinces and Germany of "Lander." All of these subdivisions fly their own flags. Most of them, however, are quite new. As a rule, these flags are never flown in ships, as only the national flag or the ensign identifies its nationality.

Nowadays many towns and cities have their own flag that uses the local colors and emblems. Many companies have also adopted corporate or "house" flags. This type of flag was developed from house flags used since the 19th century by merchant ships to identify the ship owner.

FLAG PARTS

When describing a flag it is assumed it is divided into four quarters, known as cantons. The two cantons nearest the flagpole are called the hoist, the other two are known as the fly. The upper hoist quarter is usually called the canton, except in the United States where it is called the union.

The vertical dimension of the flag is called width (but was previously known as breadth). The horizontal dimensions of the flag are called length. Most flags have dimensions with a ratio of width to length of 2:3 (Germany), or 1:2 (United Kingdom). The dimension ratio of the American Stars and Stripes is 10:19, nearly 1:2. Other national flags, such as those of Switzerland and Vatican City are 1:1, which means they are square.

The flag's field is the basic area or the background color of the flag. The field is very often a large square. The field of America's Stars and Stripes is where the 13 red and white stripes are found. Any emblem placed on the field or added to the basic design of the flag is a charge. Therefore a flag can be charged with many emblems such as a star, a crescent, a full moon, or a coat of arms, to mention just a few.

Every flag has a special sleeve at the hoist, where the rope runs through to hold it tight at the flagpole. This hoist rope often carries a toggle at the upper end and a loop, or becket at the end. When a flag is ready to be hoisted, both ends may be fitted with Inglefield Clips. These clips attach to similar devices on the halyards at the flagpole.

HERALDRY

Heraldry—the study of coats of arms—and vexillology are often mentioned together. When studying flags it is necessary to understand aspects of heraldry because some flags are charged with a coat of arms. In addition, some modern flags are based on the traditional coat of arms of a country or region.

Heraldry also uses specialist terms to describe the arms. Most significant is the use of metals and colors. The metals used are "or" (gold) and "argent" (silver). When used on a flag they are represented respectively by yellow and white.

A coat of arms is the complete heraldic device, which ideally consists of five basic elements. The most important element is the shield. In the Middle Ages, knights and soldiers carried a shield to protect themselves against assaults and attacks from the enemy. The armored knights also used the shield to identify themselves by painting their family colors and emblems on them.

The upper third of the shield, known as chief, is its most important part. The chief is often used to impart an extra, important message. The chief depicting the English lion can be found in the national flag of Fiji and represents its historical links with Britain.

Heraldic "supporters" are often used to "hold" the shield. They keep the shield in an upright position and should be seen as being able to protect it against the enemy. Supporters can be humans or species from the animal world. Lions and eagles are favorite heraldic supporters, as they are seen as the kings of the animal world. The national flag of the Republic of Moldova is charged with a shield supported by an eagle. The shield of the British Antarctic Territory, as can be seen on its flag, is supported by an English lion and a local penguin. Shield and supporters are normally placed on a compartment. This is often a mound or hill, but basically anything that can serve as solid base can be used as a compartment.

Often a scroll can be found below the shield. This is a nicely draped band of cloth, which bears an inscription, the motto. In the flag of the tiny Republic of San Marino, in Italy, the motto "Libertas" (liberty) is written on the scroll.

A crest is the heraldic device that appears above the shield, on the extreme top of the arms. In the flag of the Republic of Croatia the crest is a crown, which is made up from five small heraldic shields, which represent the original five regions of Croatia. Sometimes the crest holds mantling. These are strips of cloth,

This painting depicts three French naval ships from the 18th century. It features the French royal flag and a merchant ship of the French Merchant Navy flying a blue flag with a white cross.

casually flying or hanging from the wreath, which is a multicolored piece of rope.

FLAG COLORS

The colors most used in flags are red, white; blue, yellow, black, and green. The 1994 South African flag is the only national flag which contains them all.

These six colors are primary colors and are also used in heraldry. With the exception of black and white, these colors can be seen in all shades which is essential to distinguish one flag from another. The flags of The Netherlands and Luxembourg would be the same, were it not for the fact that Luxembourg's blue is lighter.

When used in flags, colors always carry a symbolic meaning. Red is often associated with blood and countries with a colonial history use the color red to recall the blood shed in the struggle for independence. Red is also used to symbolize revolution, socialism, and communism. White is associated with the purity of the aims of the people, often religious, and frequently also represents peace and tranquility. Blue is often used to represent water or the sky. Many nations in the Pacific region have blue flags, symbolizing the Pacific

Ocean. Several southern African countries use blue in their flags to express the importance of water and the rain to their lives.

In Islamic countries, green has a religious meaning: it was Mohammed's favorite color and is associated with hope. In Central American and African flags, green usually represents the country's vegetation or forests.

The flags of Laos and the USSR hang from buildings on a Luang Prabang street in Laos.

Yellow is seen as the color of wealth. In South American and modern African flags, yellow is usually associated with mineral wealth, especially gold. In Central America, yellow has been used to symbolize the yellow beaches and the amount of sunshine they can provide for wealthy tourists. In the flags of the Far East, yellow represents the rulers of the territories.

Black, when seen in African and Central American flags, is often associated with the people living there and their collective pride. In other flags, black recalls the tragic, dark past the country has gone through. It is used as a kind of warning sign to its people to take care of their country to avoid another dark period in their history.

Less frequently used in flags, orange features in the flags of India, Bhutan, and Sri Lanka to symbolize Hinduism. In these countries the hindu majority live with people of other faiths. The orange is always displayed with colors to represent these other religions. In Ireland, orange also has a religious meaning, representing the protestant Orangemen.

Maroon is used in the flags of the Republic of Georgia and the Gulf State of Qatar. This very dark red alludes to the color of dried blood in both flags. It represents the blood spilt in long wars of independence that has now dried since the ultimate goal has been achieved.

FLAG MATERIALS

A flag has to flutter outside in the wind, when the sun shines, and when it is raining. For this reason, the material a flag is made of has to be as weather resistant as possible. In an ideal situation a flag should be light and strong, and able to flutter freely as well as being washable, mothproof, mildew-resistant, and fire-resistant.

The first flags were made of wool. If a flag or banner was to be used by a sovereign, their envoys, or their armies, they were made of silk taffeta or silk damask. From the 13th century, the silk flags and banners were often decorated with coats of arms and other colorful designs. These were created using gold leaf, appliqué, flat stitch or chain stitch, or a combination of all these techniques. These flags were not meant for general use but were for decorative purposes only.

From the 16th century onward more flags were needed, especially for use in vessels at sea and by armies on land. These flags were embroidered or painted. Sometimes both

A line of the most famous flag in the world, the US Stars and Stripes.

techniques were employed, but painted flags were cheaper than the embroidered ones. Flags used in ships were made of wool or cheaper fabrics, such as linen and bunting. Bunting is a coarse, loosely woven fabric.

Only in the last 50 years have flag makers been able to produce flags that meet all the desirable requirements for a flag. Ideal fabrics for outdoor flags have proved to be heavyweight, two-ply polyester, or fabrics that are made of a combination of nylon and wool. Nowadays most flags are printed. Computer techniques allow flag makers to produce them on demand. There are also still flag makers where the flags are handmade by skilled workers using sewing machines.

FLAG ETIQUETTE

A flag is a symbol for a group that they are proud of. For this reason alone, a flag should be treated with respect and dignity, even if it is not the flag representing one's own group. This is a fundamental rule of flag etiquette.

There is no international overall rule that regulates flag etiquette. Most countries, however, have fixed flag laws that decree how to treat the national flag and the flags of other countries. A few countries, such as The Netherlands, do not have flag laws but their flag etiquette is based on practice.

Although there is no written universal guide for flag etiquette, there are generally accepted rules which include the following:

A flag should be treated with respect.

The flag should be displayed in the open air from sunrise to sunset. When it is flown at night it should be well illuminated and visible. It should not be hoisted in bad weather.

The flag should be hoisted briskly and lowered slowly and ceremoniously.

The flag should fly aloft and free. It should not touch the ground or any obstacle near to it. It should not be used as a seat or table cover.

The flag should not be used to write on nor should it be defaced in any other way.

Only one flag may fly from a flagpole at any time. Hoisting two or more flags from one pole is not correct.

The national flag should not be displayed in a way inferior to any other flag. When a flag is flown together with the flags of other nations, all flags should have the same dimensions and proportions. When flags of more states are involved, they should be displayed in alphabetical order, as used in the local, official language.

When three flagpoles stand together, the national flag should fly from the center pole.

Two Palestinians burn an Israeli flag while protesting at the Madrid Peace Conference.

When used as a sign of mourning, the flag is flown at half-mast. The half-mast position is to be found at circa three-quarters of the pole height.

A used flag should be burnt, but not in public.

2 The History of Flags

PRECURSORS TO THE MODERN FLAG

Since the beginning of civilization, solid flag-like objects have been used. They are called vexilloids and fulfilled the same functions as flags today. A vexilloid was a graphic symbol or totem that carried information about its owner and had a religious meaning. The oldest precursors to the modern flag were found in Mesopotamia. The Mesopotamian goddess of agriculture, Innana, is symbolized by a shepherd's crook. Later Mesopotamian deities had similar signs or badges.

In ancient Egypt, symbolic representations of the deities were very common. Horus was represented by a hawk, Anubis by a jackal, and Isis by the throne. The Egyptians were the first to attach streamers on flagpoles. Used in the precincts of the temples, they probably had no symbolic meaning and were used for decoration. On a carved mace head, from the pre-Dynastic period, a standard-like vexilloid is used to mark the presence of a king. Another example from the 12th century BC exemplifies how a standard marks a division of an army.

It is very doubtful that vexilloids were used as national symbols in Ancient Egypt, but symbols were gradually introduced. The Babylonian stele of Ur Nammu (c. 2100 BC) shows two emblems, depicting a crescent moon and a sun, symbolizing the sun god Shamash. These totem emblems are still used as symbols. First nations in North America still make use of totems, carved out of wood.

Emblems of a more national character were acquired when trade and warfare took to the seas. The Phoenicians were the first to put flagstaffs on their galleys. These poles bore the crescent and disc of the moon-goddess Astare, as well as decorative streamers.

The Romans also used vexilloids attached to what might be called a flagstaff. Each Roman legion had a staff with an "aquila," an eagle, and each cohort carried its own "signum." This consisted of a staff, topped with a crosspiece carrying representations of various animals. Each detached unit to a cohort had a vexillum (standard), made of fabric. Their earliest use dates from about the fourth century BC. The auxiliary cavalry used the draco, a dragon-shape standard and the imago, the Emperor's portrait.

The Romans had another fabric flag called a flammula: a spear on which several red streamers were attached. It is thought it was used to mark the presence of the general. The Romans also introduced the labarum, a fabric flag derived from the vexillum, during Christian times. The labarum was made of purple cloth and showed the image of the Emperor and his family.

THE FORERUNNERS OF FLAGS

There are strong signs that the ancient Chinese used flags in the way that they are used today. They were the first to make cloth out of silk and this strong, lightweight fabric made excellent flags. The first reference to such a flag dates to 1122 BC, when a white flag announced the presence of the Emperor of the Chou Dynasty.

From China, the practice of attaching flags laterally to poles traveled to the Mediterranean. Although we know that Muslims used this kind of flag as they stormed through the Middle East, nobody knows exactly what kind of flags the Islamic armies used.

On the Christian side, in the early Middle Ages, the practice grew of bestowing banners that had been blessed by the Pope. These

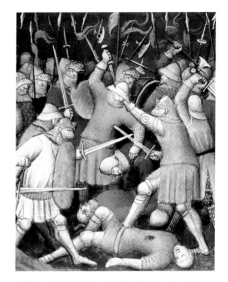

An illustration depicting the Fifth Christian Crusade.

banners, called "pallia," were originally garments. Among those to have received a pallia were Charlemagne, St Augustine, and William the Conqueror. No exact description has survived, but it is believed that one is depicted in the famous Bayeux Tapestry. This illustrates a flag-like object used as a mark of identification on land. A similar style influenced the design of the new flag of the Channel Island of Guernsey in 1985.

It is certain that the Vikings used flags in their ships to identify themselves. The raven standard is mentioned several times in Nordic literature. Harold Hardrada, who invaded England in 1066, had a banner called "landeytha," or the "landwaster." We also owe the word flag to the Normans. It is derived from the old Saxon or Germanic words "fflake" or "ffleogan," which both mean fly or flap in the wind. A "flag" therefore means that a piece of fabric is freely fluttering in the wind.

A turning point in the history of flags was the development of heraldry. Traditionally, heraldry originates at the start of the First Crusade in 1095. There were two reasons for this. Firstly, the Christian pilgrims needed a sign or a badge to show they were on a crusade. The second reason was a knight wore armor that covered his face making him anonymous. Heraldry was used to "name" the knight by the use of colors and emblems.

The first badge of the Crusades was the Christian cross. This was displayed by the Crusaders on the front and back of their surcoats and was also used on pennants and flags. In 1188, at the start of the Third Crusade, it was agreed that Crusaders of different nationalities would have different crosses. The Flemings, for example, were allocated green crosses.

A later development was that different colors became associated with patron saints or with military religious orders. This practice became widespread and the crosses and colors were transferred to heraldic coats of arms. The English patron St. George became associated with a red cross on a white background, while the Scottish patron St. Andrew was identified by a white saltire on a blue background. There is no doubt that flags bearing crosses, such as the Danish, English, and pre-revolutionary French flags, originate from the Crusades. Other flags, such as those of Sweden, Norway, Quebec, and Switzerland are indirectly derived from the Crusades.

These signs, as shown on military uniforms and armor, eventually became commonly used on pieces of fabric. Attached to a staff or pole they could be held in the air. On the battlefields it became easier to recognize who was friend and who was foe.

As the Middle Ages progressed, the heraldic devices became more complicated. Original coats of arms were simple and symbolized the heritage and possessions of their owner. Gradually these arms became more complex, as their owners wished to express more about themselves, revealing parentage and land claims. Shown on the heraldic shields, these complex images were more difficult to paint or embroider on flags.

At the same time, the use of heraldic banners to show nationality became restricted to the monarch and his appointed agents.

SEA FLAGS

Ships from western European countries began to explore the world from the end of the 15th century. When these ships were privately owned, they were not allowed to use heraldic banners to show their nationality, as these were restricted to the monarch and his agents. They had to find another solution—this came from The Netherlands.

In 1568, the Spanish ruled The Netherlands from Madrid. The Dutch at that time had converted to Protestantism, but the Catholic Spanish found this unacceptable. Under Prince William of Orange, the Dutch

An illustration showing the ship belonging to the explorer, pirate, and navigator, Sir Francis Drake flying a flag with the cross of St. George and a standard.

THE VALIANT EXPLOITS OF SIR FRANCIS DRAKE, 1587.

revolted against Spain. They used ships during raids but could not fly the banner of the Spanish king so they invented a flag which could be easily recognized as a sign of revolt. The Prinsenvlag, as this revolutionary flag was called, had three horizontal stripes of orange, white, and blue. The colors showed that Prince William of Orange (orange stripe) was protector of religious freedom (white and blue stripes). Blue and white had been used as symbols of Christianity during the Middle Ages.

The Dutch set the trend for simpler designs. At sea they had the advantage that their flags were easily recognizable. Ships owned by the monarch, or in his service, still used complicated flags; normally they were of a single color, with the complete coat of arms painted or embroidered.

The next development in sea flags was the creation of what might be called "house" flags. England, as well as The Netherlands, had companies whose aims were to establish trading links with other places around the world. The English Guinea Company used a flag based on that of St. George. The flags of the Muscovy Company and the Cathay Company showed a combination of the St. George cross with the British royal arms. These company (house) flags, identified their

ships while trading. The Dutch East India Company (VOC) was set up in 1602 by the revolutionary government, so the house flag was based on the Prinsenvlag and it was charged with the VOC logo in its central white stripe.

As commercial sea trade expanded across Western Europe, more flags came into widespread use. Ships flew not only their national flag but also showed regional or city colors. French sea towns produced many blue and white flags, while the Northern European Hansa cities often used red and white flags. Examples of early modern flag usage can be found in paintings from the 16th and 17th centuries when the sea trade was booming.

FLAG CHARTS

A large number of flag books and charts were produced from the 17th century onward and this reflects the role assigned to flags at sea. As an increasing number of flags were deployed, it became more difficult to identify them. Books and charts served as handy reference works.

Early flag books were sketchbooks, in which interested people made drawings of the flags they saw or of which they had heard.

The first flag book, known in short as *Libro de Conoscimento*, was handwritten and illuminated in about 1350 by an anonymous Franciscan friar. It shows a map of the then known world on which the coastal cities are identified with heraldic banners: none of these banners are in use anymore. However, when Abkhazia broke away from the former Soviet Republic of Georgia in 1992, it adopted a flag design based on that used for its territory in this 14th century flag book.

The first modern flag collections are from The Netherlands. The Gortter Manuscript, dating from about 1600, holds a collection of hand-painted banners used by the Dutch revolutionary regiments fighting against Spain. In the second half of the 17th century, captains of ships began to develop a real interest in flags flown by other ships at sea. Several Dutch, English, and French manuscripts have survived, which illustrate the flags seen by these seafarers.

The most influential flag book of that period was *Nieuwe Hollandse Scheeps-Bouw*, first published in 1694 by Carel Allard in Amsterdam. The book deals with shipbuilding but also has a large section on flags showing the importance of those flown on ships. Allard's black and white drawings were copied in other flag books and charts.

The first flag chart, called *Table des pavillons quil'on arbore dans toute les Parties du Monde Connu, Consernant la Marine,* was printed in Amsterdam in about 1700. Edited and printed by Cornelius Danckerts, the flags were colored by hand. The title in French—the international language at that time—indicates that these charts were meant to be used internationally.

Many flag charts and books have been published since these first attempts to systemize and catalog flags. The first official charts came into print in France in 1858. Captain Le Gras' *Album des Pavillons, Guidons, Flammes, de toutes les Puissances Maritimes* was published in full color by the Secretary of State for use by the French Imperial Navy. Le Gras used information collected from official government sources around the world. Each French naval vessel had such a book on board.

In 1868, the American Bureau of Navigation began publication of the official flag book, *Flags of Maritime Nations from the Most Authentic Sources.* In the United Kingdom, George Hounsell produced *Flags and Signals of All Nations* in 1874, with the approval of the Admiralty. Now a standard work known as BR20, it is still updated for use by the British Navy.

TODAY'S NATIONAL FLAGS

With American independence (1776) and the French Revolution (1789), the concept of the modern nation state was born and this exerted an influence on the design and use of flags. Whereas flags had mainly been used at sea before these historical turning points, now they were used to express political aspirations and the flag became a rallying point. People knew they would find brothers and sisters with the same ideals under a particular flag as the flag expressed their mutual political ideals.

During the French Revolution, the French blue flag with heraldic lilies was seen as a symbol of the old order. The will to change to a better world was represented by the new flag, the Tricolore. The old royal French flag had been difficult to produce but this new revolutionary flag could be sewn easily and quickly.

At the turn of the 19th century, the world was roughly divided into several multi-ethnic Empires. Those who felt oppressed by their foreign rulers gradually became aware that they could do take the same steps as the Americans and French several decades before. They started fighting for independence. In the first half of the 19th century, Central and South America were at the forefront of this fight and they designed flags to express their ambitions. The resulting flags were inspired by their political role models of France and the United States. The trend was now set: more countries emerged from empires and new nations states were born, beginning in Europe in the Balkans.

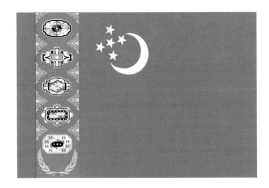

Turkmenistan flag

Risings against traditional and authoritarian rule took place in several parts of Europe during the Revolution Year, 1848. These uprisings were echoes of the French Revolution decades before and new tricolors were carried aloft. The German black, red, and yellow flag was adopted that year to symbolize the creation of a new nation state out of many tiny kingdoms, duchies, and principalities. The flags of the Irish Republic and Hungary were first displayed during the Revolution Year.

In December 1865, the British Secretary of State for the Colonies ordered all colonial vessels of war to wear a blue ensign with the badge or the seal of the colony in the fly. The order led to the development of many new flags, subsequently used on land to represent each colony, such as those of the Australian states. Some are still in use today, despite changes to colonial status.

The 20th century saw the birth of the vast majority of current national flags. It began in Australia and New Zealand, where each had obtained a high level of autonomy. Both adopted flags which symbolized their alliance with Britain. After World War I, new countries emerged from Empires that had fallen apart, such as the Austrian-Hungarian, the Ottoman Empire, and Russia. Every new country

adopted its own flag, often newly designed, with colors and emblems found in the local history. One such state was Czechoslovakia, which found inspiration in the use of the pan-Slavic colors of white, blue, and red.

Another new flag that emerged from World War I was the Red Flag. It was introduced after the October 1918 Revolution in Russia, which was then being built into a new empire, the Soviet Union. This red flag inspired old and new nations who saw socialism and communism as their state "religion," including the People's Republic of China.

World War II was the prelude to the penultimate boom in the birth of nations and flags. At the end of the war, the world counted some 60 nation states which all applied for membership of the United Nations. France and Great Britain ruled half of the world at that time. Yet a steady process of emancipation from colonial rule had begun. Starting with India and Pakistan in 1947, colonies in Asia, Africa, Central America, and Oceania achieved independence. Most flags of these new countries were designed from scratch. Many of them, however, were inspired by existing designs. Several governments, particularly those in the Caribbean and Oceania, organized flag design competitions.

The winners are remembered and revered for having created a tradition.

The last new flag boom was seen in the final decade of the 20th century. From the collapsed, multi-ethnic states of the Soviet Union and Yugoslavia emerged some 20 new countries. About half of them had historical flags, which were used as the base for the new national flag. The flags of the other new nations had to be created. Once more colors and emblems were found in the local history books. One of the countries to create a new flag was Turkmenistan. It found emblems among its tribes who produced the country's famous carpets and five of these tribes now find their traditional guls, or carpet designs, on the national flag.

FLAGS OF THE FUTURE

The world currently consists of 192 flag-flying independent countries. As their independence is not disputed, all but one (Vatican City) of them are member states of the United Nations. The latest country to see its flag flying in front of the UN building in New York is East Timor, near Indonesia. Its flag was based on that of the political party that led the struggle for independence.

There are several countries that act as completely independent countries, but are not recognized as such by the rest of the world. The most famous example is Taiwan, an island off the Chinese coast, officially called the Republic of China. The communist-ruled People's Republic of China does not recognize its government. The Taiwanese flag is one China originally adopted in 1928 and it is based on the party flag of the nationalistic Kuomingtang Party.

The northern parts of Cyprus and of Somalia act as though they are independent and proudly fly their own flags. After the decline of the Soviet Union in 1991, several new countries emerged which are not internationally recognized, including Transdnestria, Artsakh, and Abkhazia. Other aspirant nations, seeking independence under their own flags, have founded the Unrepresented Nations and Peoples Organisation (UNPO) in The Hague (Netherlands). The flags of these would-be states are displayed in the UNPO office. Around the world, peoples wanting autonomy or independence have developed their own flags. One example is Quebec, where there is a strong movement in favor of self-determination in this French-speaking Canadian province.

The people of Quebec feel strongly about their flag, as a symbol of potential independence from Canada.

A national flag represents an entire nation, so everybody must feel happy with the design and its symbolism. Only Tonga has laid down in its constitution that its flag shall never be changed. All other countries leave this option open. It is fairly certain that some of them will change their flag in the future. As political aspirations change this will be reflected in the flag designs. In Canada, the colonial-style flag was not popular with all groups so it was changed to its current design in 1965. It has become one of the simplest and most striking of national flags.

One of the nations that might alter its flag in the future is Australia. There is a strong movement, not supported by the majority, to remove the colonial past (a miniature version of the UK's Union Jack) from the flag. A growing number of people argue that Australia has become a nation of its own and should have a pure Australian flag. A similar argument is also gaining ground in New Zealand.

The flag history of Africa has seen many changes since the start of the process of decolonization in the 1960s. Political aspirations can change suddenly with a coup d'état or the installation of a new president. Such changes are often reflected in a new national flag. Africa has seen dozens of new flags as a result of political changes; Angola, Mozambique, and Malawi have announced that a flag change is due to reflect the current political situation in their countries.

Thanks to modern communication techniques, flags at sea have lost their importance. However, they are still used to identify the ship's nationality, although they are no longer flown in abundance as in early seafaring days. The world has never seen as many flags as it has today. They have become popular signs of identification on land, showing who we are and what we like others to know about us.

3 Flag Families

The flags of the world can be divided into roughly nine families. A flag "family" is a group of flags with similar origins or designs. Sometimes the relationship between different flags is very obvious, such as the flags used in the Arab countries. In other cases it is not so clear that one flag has emerged from another flag.

CHRISTIAN CROSSES

The cross has not always been the symbol of Christianity; originally it was a fish. The cross on which Christ died became a Christian emblem during the Crusades of the 11th century. Pilgrims to the Holy Land decorated themselves with the cross to proclaim their mission. This emblem was later put on heraldic banners, which developed into flags. Nearly all flags bearing crosses originate directly or indirectly from this period. Crosses are no longer seen as strictly Christian emblems, but they are now emblems in their own right.

The Scots and Danes argue over whose flag is the oldest. Both think God gave them their flag on the battlefield, while fighting a religious war. The Scots believe this happened near the village of Athelstaneford in AD 832. In a blue sky they saw an x-shaped cloud formation after they had prayed for help and it was seen as a sign that God was on the side of the Scottish.

It is the belief of the Danes that God personally sent the flag to the battlefield in Estonia in 1219. The Danes were losing the battle against the pagan Estonians, when they prayed to God for victory. God gave his blessing by sending the flag down. This was the battle's turning point.

It was not until 1625 that the Danish flag, named Dannebrog, was adopted as the official national flag of that country. In those days, the Danes had a wide influence in Northern Europe. Sweden was the first country to adopt a flag that was based on the Dannebrog. Their design became known as the Scandinavian Cross. Norway, Finland, and Iceland also used the Scandinavian Cross in their flags and several regions in the northern part of Europe, which seek autonomy or independence, have also adopted it in their flags.

Three crosses are to be found in the flag of the United Kingdom. This Union Flag is a combination of the crosses and saltires of the Christian patron saints of England (St. George

The Danes believe their flag was sent down by God.

Cross), Scotland (St. Andrew Cross), and Ireland (St. Patrick Cross). This design has influenced many other flags in the world, such as those of the British dependencies. The St. George Cross was an honor bestowed on the island of Malta in World War II and it became part of the flag. However, the merchant flag of this island republic in the Mediterranean shows the typical Maltese Cross, which represents four spearheads laid together as a cross.

There are several other flags bearing crosses. Switzerland is named after its oldest canton, Schwyz, and modeled its national flag on the cross flag of Schwyz which originated from the Crusades. The flag of the Kingdom of Tonga in the Pacific carries a cross, which illustrates that the island people there converted to Christianity.

THE MUSLIM CRESCENT

The crescent is one of the oldest emblems in the world. It was used in the ancient precursors of flags. What the cross is to Christians, the crescent moon has become to Muslims. Most of the countries where Islam is the main religion fly flags charged with a crescent, often accompanied by at least one star. The crescent represents the waxing moon. As it is grows to become a full moon, the crescent expresses the will of the people to become wise adults who, at the same time, still have a long way to go and much to learn.

The crescent is mentioned in the 53rd surah (chapter) of the Koran. The first evidence of the crescent moon as a Muslim emblem can be found on the so-called "portolano" flag charts dating from the late Middle Ages. They show crescents used as emblems for the kings of Damascus (yellow with a white crescent), Cairo (white with a blue crescent), and Tunis (white with a black crescent). Another Muslim sign used in those early days was the "Hand of Fatima," the daughter of the Prophet Muhammad, and the split sword of Ali, known as z'l-faqar.

The Turks were able to build up a vast empire, to become known as the Ottoman Empire. They adopted the crescent sign, which soon after became the main symbol of Islam. In the 16th century, the Turks started using flags showing three crescents. This type of flag came into widespread use across the Islamic world. In the beginning, crescents were not accompanied by stars. A star as an additional Islamic emblem was first introduced in 1793. The Turks popularized the use of the crescent and star.

At the collapse of the Ottoman Empire after World War I, Turkey adopted a red flag with a white crescent and star. At that time the country was seen as a role model by several Muslim nations in Northern Africa and Asia. After achieving independence they all incorporated the crescent into their flags. Indonesia, which has the world's largest Muslim population, is among the few Islamic countries, which does not have a crescent on its flag.

CELESTIAL BODIES

Celestial bodies, such as the sun, moon, and stars, feature in many national flags of all continents. In ancient times, celestial bodies inspired people and were more a part of everyday life. The sun, moon, and stars are still universally seen as emblems to express deep feelings. Where these celestial bodies are not used as symbols on the flag, they may be referred to in the meaning of one or more colors.

Sun

No one will argue that without the sun there would be no life on earth. The sun is associated, therefore, with life and strength. Among the countries that refer to the sun as the bringer of all life are Chad, Guinea-Bissau, and Gabon in Africa, and Jamaica, St Kitts-Nevis, and Trinidad and Tobago in the Caribbean. The sun is mostly represented by the use of yellow. However, the red fields in Trinidad and Tobago's flag represent the sun.

The flags of Argentina and Uruguay are charged with representations of the sun called the "Sun of May." They recall the fact that the sun started shining when independence was declared, which was seen as a good omen. The sun is also given a prominent position in the flag of Antigua and Barbuda—a rising sun symbolizes the dawn of a new era for the islands.

The name of the African country Malawi means "flaming waters," which refers to the color of the sun when mirrored in Lake Nyasa. The sun is honored with a central position on the flag. The sun in Namibia's flag represents life and energy. In the Rwandan flag it represents the light that guides all people. The flag of Taiwan is said to represent "a white sun in a blue sky over red land." The sun was the emblem of the Kuomingtang, the Chinese Nationalist Party, which came into power in 1928. In this flag the sun has 12 rays, each one represents two hours of the day.

Moon

The moon, which is traditionally associated with femininity, features in two positions in the flags of the world. As mentioned above, a waxing moon in the Muslim world symbolizes Islam. The full moon is depicted on the flag of the island republic of Palau in the Pacific. The Palauans believe this phase of the moon is the best time for planting, harvesting, tree-felling, fishing, and carving traditional canoes. It is the optimum time for human activity.

Stars

Stars have been used for navigation purposes since ancient times. Portugal was once a nation which explored the globe and it recalls that past history with the representation of an armillary sphere—an early navigational tool—in its flag.

Stars are usually represented with five points, but not always. The Americans first introduced stars as flag emblems. They served to represent the members of a new "constellation" of states. Since first featured in the American flag of 1776, the star emblem has been copied all over the world. In the Stars and Stripes, as the flag of the United States of America is known, the number of stars indicates how many states are admitted to the Union.

The practice of using a number of stars to equal the number of member states or provinces of a country is also used in the flag of Brazil. In 1992, the number of stars was increased to 27 after two new states were admitted to the Federation.

Some countries represent different parts of their country as stars on the flag, such as

A starry night has been the inspiration for many flag designs, with stars featuring in flags all over the world.

the island states of the Comoros, Cape Verde, São Tomé, and Príncipe in Africa, and the Federated States of Micronesia and Tuvalu in the Pacific. The stars in the flag of Honduras recall the number of Central American states united with Honduras between 1821 and 1839.

The Southern Cross, or Crux Australis, is the most prominent constellation in the Southern Hemisphere and is visible throughout the year. The Southern Cross consists of five stars, and has been used as a navigational aid for centuries, starting with European ships exploring trade links. The constellation became a popular emblem for new settlers in South America and the Far East. During the time it was a British colony, the Australian state of Victoria was the first to show the Southern Cross in its flag in 1870. It is found in the current flags of Australia, New Zealand, Papua New Guinea, Samoa, and also features in the Brazilian national flag, among other constellations. Alaska's state flag shows the most conspicuous constellation of the Northern Hemisphere, the Plough, also known as the Great Bear.

A star often accompanies the crescent in the flags of Muslim countries. This is a representation of Venus, known as the Morning star, which is the brightest star in the sky. The star together with a crescent was introduced as an Islamic emblem at the end of the 18th century.

In the flags of many modern nations, a single star usually represents unity. This may mean different things. It might represent the call for unity of different people living in a country (Suriname), or express the wish that all tribes will unite to build one nation state (Somalia).

In socialist-ruled states the star, often red, symbolizes communism. Since the red flag of socialism was lowered in 1991 after the collapse of the Soviet Union, the star of communism can still be seen in the flags of the People's Republic of China and North Korea.

THE UNION FLAG OF GREAT BRITAIN

After King James VI of Scotland inherited the English throne in 1603, he became King James I of both England and Scotland, although the two countries still remained independent. As a result of this, English ships displayed the flag of St. George (white with a red cross) and the Scottish vessels flew the flag of St. Andrew (blue with a white saltire)—often in the canton of plain or striped flags.

Soon confusion arose over the flags flown by naval and merchant vessels of both England and Scotland. King James wanted a flag to express the Union and on April 12, 1606, he issued a proclamation declaring:

"That from henceforth all our subjects of this Island and Kingdome of Great Britaine, and the Members thereof, shall bear in their Maintoppe the Red Crosse, commonly called S. Georges Crosse, and the White Crosse, commonly called S. Andrews Crosse, joined together, according to a forme made by our Heralds."

The "Maintoppe" was the top of the ship's main sail. In the foretop sail the English or the Scottish flag would still be flown. This proclamation is the birth certificate of the Union Flag, which was to become one of the best-known flags in the world.

This first version of the Union Flag was flown until 1634, when King James' proclamation was repealed, after disputes concerning saluting ships in the Channel. The use of the Union Flag was then restricted to the king's own ships or those in his service. Merchant ships were no longer permitted to fly the Union Flag and had to revert to their "old" English and Scottish flags.

With the execution of Charles I on January 30, 1649, the union of England and Scotland came to an end. The Union Flag was lowered until after a new union with Scotland (April 12, 1654) when it was readopted in May 1660. The United Kingdom of Great Britain came into existence on May 1, 1707, with the parliamentary union of England and Scotland. The first article of the Treaty decreed that the Union Flag would be the crosses of St. George and St. Andrew conjoined in such a manner as the Queen decided. Queen Anne chose to keep the existing design as the national flag of the United Kingdom. This was then added as cantons to the different types of ensigns in use, as well as in the three Naval squadron flags.

On January 1, 1801, Ireland became part of the United Kingdom and was represented in the flag by a red saltire to represent the island. This saltire is commonly known as St. Patrick's Cross. However, St. Patrick was not martyred and is never represented by a cross. It was in fact the emblem of the powerful Irish Fitzgerald family. No change to the Union Flag was made in 1921, when the southern part of Ireland became independent.

From the early 17th century, the Royal Navy was divided into a red, white, or blue squadrons. These vessels flew ensigns in the color of their squadron, with the St. George Cross in the canton. With the abolition of the

The "Union Jack" has been around since the 1600s and it is still featured in many flags around the world today, showing Britain's colonial past.

squadronal division of the Navy on July 9, 1864, the red, blue, and white ensigns became free for other purposes. The white ensign was assigned to the Navy. The red ensign became the national colors for all British ships—basically merchant vessels and privately owned yachts. Civil vessels could only fly a defaced red ensign if they received permission from the Admiralty, which dealt with flag issues. The Admiralty issued special warrants to Canada (1892), New Zealand (1899), and Australia (1903), as well as to several other countries, which are now independent.

Under the Colonial Naval Defence Act of 1865, colonial governments were allowed to use the blue ensign with a badge in the fly. This Act led to the enormous growth of blue ensigns defaced by badges. These flags are used on land today in the dozen or so remaining British dependencies, such as the Cayman Islands, St Helena, and Montserrat. In the flag of Hawaii, the Union Flag recalls the friendly relationship between the UK and Hawaii in the 19th century. Though they are now independent, the countries of Australia, New Zealand, Tuvalu, and Fiji in Oceania still fly old colonial-style flags.

THE STARS AND STRIPES
OF AMERICA

From the beginning of the 16th century, North America was colonized by European settlers. Virginia was the first English colony in what would become known as the New World, but the Dutch also played an important role in the early colonization of North America. Merchant ships from both countries brought flags, using the colors red, white, and blue. Among these flags was that of the British East India Company, which was red-and-white striped with the British Union Flag in the canton.

Although no written evidence has survived, it is apparent that this flag played a significant role in the development of the Stars and Stripes. At about the time armed conflicts between Great Britain and its American subjects broke out in April 1775, a merchant flag came into use, having 13 alternating red and white stripes.

The flag hoisted by General George Washington at Prospect Hill in Massachusetts on January 1, 1776, also had 13 stripes, but with the British Union Flag in the canton. The flag was called the Grand Union flag or the Continental Colors. It was basically the same

The US flag, the Stars and Stripes, blowing in the wind. It originally featured the British Union Flag in the canton, until it achieved independence in 1777.

flag as that of the British East India Company. The small Union Flag in the canton expressed the existing loyalty to Britain.

Thirteen colonies declared independence from Great Britain on July 4, 1776. They had no official flag. That came by Resolution of the Continental Congress on June 14, 1777, which stated:

"Resolved, that the Flag of the United States be 13 stripes alternate red and white, that the Union be 13 stars white in a blue field representing a new constellation."

The earlier representation of the Union Flag in the canton was now changed to an "American" blue field with 13 stars. From that date there were two different designs of the American flag. Francis Hopkinson's design shows the stars in five vertical rows, while the so-called Betsy Ross design has the stars in a circle. One of the earliest accounts of the flag is that of Alfred B. Street. In October 1777, he saw Betsy Ross' design in Saratoga, where the British general Burgoyne surrendered. Street wrote:

"The stars were disposed in a circle, symbolizing the perpetuity of the Union; the ring, like the circling serpent of the Egyptians, signifying eternity. The thirteen stripes showed with the stars the number of the United colonies, and denoted the subordination of the

States to the Union, as well as equality among themselves."

Great Britain recognized American independence on November 30, 1782. This peace allowed other North American territories to join the Union. By 1818 the Union had grown to 20 states, which all had to be represented in the flag. Twenty alternating red and white stripes, however, would make the Stars and Stripes very complicated. In the Flag Act of April 4, 1818, it was decided that the new flag would have 13 stripes and 20 stars:

"And be it further enacted, that on the admission of every new State into the Union, one star shall be added to the union of the flag; such addition shall take effect on the fourth of July next succeeding such admission."

Since then, as more states have joined the Union, there have been 27 different flags. The last time the Stars and Stripes was altered was on July 4, 1960, to welcome Hawaii as the 50th state.

During the American Civil War of 1861–1865, the South ceded from the Union and created its own flag. However, these were modeled on the flag of the country they broke away from. The first flag of the South had three horizontal bands of red, white, and red, with a blue canton with seven white stars. These later increased to 13 as more states joined the Confederacy. The second flag of the South—the so-called Battle Flag—was a red flag with a white and blue saltire, charged with 13 stars.

Other countries have looked to the design and symbolism of the American flag when creating their own. Chile adopted a flag based on the American flag, in October 1817, designed by an American artist who fought with the Chilean freedom fighters. In 1822 Greece chose a flag that looked very similar to the American flag. It created a striped flag with a canton displaying a cross instead of stars. The canton is considered the most important part of the flag, as it remains visible when the flag is not flying in the wind. Other countries that modeled their flags on the American flag were Liberia (1847), Cuba (1848), Uruguay (1830), and Panama (1903).

Modern flags are still using it, including those of Malaysia (1950), Togo (1960), and Abkhazia (1992). Several flags of American states and dependencies are closely modeled on the Stars and Stripes. Among these are the banners of Texas, Tennessee, North Carolina, Wyoming, Guam, American Samoa, and Puerto Rico.

The Americans had fought the British in the 18th century for liberty and democracy. The Stars and Stripes represented those ideals and therefore became a symbol for other oppressed people who were struggling for their own liberty and for democratic values.

THE FRENCH FLAG

The French Revolution began on July 14, 1789, with the attack on the royal fortress of the Bastille in Paris. The Tricolore was not used that day but is perceived as the flag of the republican movement. It was not used as the French national flag until February 15, 1794.

Before the Revolution, France did not have a national flag. It was ruled by the Bourbon dynasty, which used mainly white flags. Other flags used in ships were blue with a white cross. The day before the attack on the Bastille, the Paris militia were issued with blue and red cockades. Cockades were like ties, which were pinned onto coats. Blue and red were the city colors of Paris, used in the municipal coat of arms.

Three days after the attack on the Bastille, the French King Louis XVI was given such a cockade by the Marquis de Lafayette and attached it onto his own white one. Lafayette, who had been a commander of French troops in America, suggested that a cockade in blue, white, and red should become the "colors of liberty." This was agreed on October 4, 1789.

At the time of the revolution, flags were not so important as they are today and they were mainly used in ships. The French naval ships were the first to use a streamer in the "colors of liberty," attached to the royal white flag. This did not satisfy the revolutionary sailors. On October 24, 1790, the white naval ensign was charged with a tricolor canton.

The new Republic was declared on September 22, 1792, and moves were made to further eliminate the Bourbon white. On February 15, 1794, the Tricolore, consisting of three vertical stripes of blue, white, and red, was adopted as the national French flag.

The French ideas of liberty, equality, and fraternity spread across the world and the Tricolore became a symbol for people with the same ideals. France, led by Napoleon, took its new freedom to neighboring parts of Europe by military force. Napoleon helped the unification of Italy, which started in August 1796 in the Northern Italian town of Reggio. On November 6, 1796, he gave out colors of green, white, and red to the new Lombard Legion in Milan. The vertical arrangement of the colors showed it was a variation on the French flag. As the state of Italy changed, the flag kept its current shape.

French football fans celebrate the World Cup in 1998.

Italy's example inspired revolutionary leaders of independence movements to create flags with vertical arrangements of colors. This happened in Mexico (1815), Belgium (1831), Ireland (1848), and Romania (1867). Most of the former French colonies in Africa adopted vertical striped flags at independence, as a tribute to France.

France and its revolutionary ideals are not always symbolized by the use of flags with a vertical color arrangement. Sometimes the use of the blue, white, and red serve the same purpose. Norway used the French colors in its national flag, as did Paraguay (1811), the Dominican Republic (1844), and Costa Rica (1848). In the Caribbean, Haiti recalls its French past by the use of red and blue. In 1804, it stripped the white to symbolize that it had broken with France.

THE PAN-SLAV COLORS
White, blue, and red

Czar Alexei Romanov decreed on April 9, 1667, that the Russian colors were to be white, blue, and red. They were the livery or city colors of Moscow and were first used in the merchant ship *Orjol*. Alexei's son, Czar Peter the Great, was anxious to build his own imperial navy to secure his borders. He relied heavily on foreign expertise in this field and during 1697–1698 traveled incognito, as "Peter Mikhailov," to The Netherlands and England to learn how to build ships.

Back in Russia, Peter the Great built up a Russian navy. The new vessels needed flags, so in 1699 he created a special naval flag, white with a blue saltire. At the same time, he decreed that the Russian flag flown by merchant vessels was to be the one his father had chosen. It has been the national flag on land ever since. After the Russian Revolution of 1918, and until August 1991, it was replaced by the socialist red flag.

The Italian flag followed the pattern of the French Tricolore, using the colors of red, white, and green instead.

It is sometimes suggested that Peter the Great copied the Dutch flag but changed the color arrangement, to acknowledge that the Dutch had taught him how to build a navy. During his first visit to Holland however, the white, blue, and red Russian flag was already in use.

Pan-Slavism started at the beginning of the 18th century among Slavic people in Eastern Europe, which was ruled by the Ottoman, Hungarian, and Austrian empires. These people saw the Russians as their protectors, as they were Slavic people who had been able to build a vast empire. The Russian colors became a symbol for Slavic demands for autonomy. In about 1835, Serbia was the first to arrange the Russian colors in a different order—red, blue, and white.

The first pan-Slav Congress was held in Prague in 1848, the European Year of Revolution. Slavic people living in the Austrian Empire, such as Czechs, Croats, and Slovaks, attended. These provinces of the Austrian Empire had adopted similar pan-Slav tricolors at the time of the Congress. Slovakia boldly copied the Russian flag, while Croatia copied the Dutch color arrangement.

Montenegro adopted the pan-Slav colors at the end of the 19th century with a copy of the flag of Serbia. Bulgaria's flag of 1878 was also based on the pan-Slav colors. It changed the blue stripe to green, to avoid being a plain copy of the Russian flag. Green was meant to represent hope and energy.

After World War I, the southern Slav states merged into what became known as Yugoslavia. The national flag of this multi-ethnic state was also in the pan-Slav colors and from 1945 until 1992 it was charged with the socialist red star. Montenegro and Serbia, which constitute today's Yugoslavia, fly the same red, blue, and white flag. When declaring independence in the early 1990s, the people of Croatia and Slovenia chose their national flags in these pan-Slav colors. When Czechoslovakia split into the Czech Republic and Slovakia, these new counties kept their pan-Slav colors to remember their heritage.

THE PAN-ARAB COLORS
White, black, green, and red

The oldest Arab flags were plain red. However, most Arabs lived in the Ottoman Empire and so used a red flag with a crescent and star. Before World War I, there was a move toward pan-Arabism, as Arabs were seeking more autonomy within the Ottoman Empire.

Searching for identifying "Arab" colors, a literary club of young Arabs decided on a flag with four colors in 1911. Apart from the historic red, they chose white, black, and green. The poet Safi al-Din al-Hili explained the symbolism of the four colors: "White is our deeds, Black is our battles, Green is our fields, Red is our knives."

The Arab Revolt against Ottoman rule began in Hijaz on June 10, 1916, under a plain red flag. The leader of the revolt, Sharif Hussein of Mecca, hoisted the first flag using pan-Arab colors nearly a year later, on May 30, 1917. At the fall of the Ottoman Empire after World War I, the Arab territories were divided between France and the United Kingdom. The whole region was in turmoil at that time, which led to the creation of pan-Arab flags, using several different color arrangements and designs. The oldest remaining pan-Arab flag is that of Jordan, which was introduced in 1921.

It was not until the end of World War II, however, that most of the Arab countries became independent and chose flags using the pan-Arab colors. National flags using the pan-Arab colors are Syria (1980), Jordan (1921), Oman (1970), United Arab Emirates (1971), Kuwait (1961), and Iraq (1963). Palestine, Somaliland, and the Western Sahara, which are seeking independence, have also adopted the pan-Arab colors.

PAN-AFRICAN COLORS
Red, yellow, green, and black

Ethiopia was never colonized by a European power. It is the oldest independent African state and has one of the longest flag histories in Africa. This began in about 1894 when red, yellow, and green army streamers were made into one flag. A national Ethiopian flag was first flown in Europe in 1898, when an official delegation visited Paris.

In 1917 Marcus Garvey created a black, red, and green flag for the United Negro Improvement Association. Garvey promoted the "Back to Africa" movement and saw the colors red, yellow, and green as those of the Negro state, which would be established in Africa. The colors became associated with the Black Power movement in the United States of America and in the Caribbean.

Garvey influenced a number of prominent African politicians after World War II. Independence movements adopted the pan-African colors. When Ghana became independent as the first modern African state in 1957, it chose a flag in the combined Ethiopian and Garvey colors. A dozen or so other African and Caribbean countries followed this example when they gained independence. Among them are Cameroon (1957), Guinea (1958), Guyana (1966), and Zimbabwe (1980).

4 International Flags

Most flags represent one single group of people. There are, however, some flags which represent several groups of people. These are the international flags. The flags of the Red Cross and the Red Crescent societies, as well as that of the United Nations, are respected as peace symbols around the world. Some other international flags only have a regional importance.

UNITED NATIONS

Almost every country in the world has joined the United Nations (UN), whose main aim is peace around the world. The UN was founded on October 24, 1945, and it had 51 founder members. UN forces have since been on peace

missions in all parts of the world and take the UN flag with them. The light blue flag is one of the most respected flags in the world.

The Presentation Branch of the US Office of Strategic Services (the forerunner of the CIA) was asked in April 1945 to design a logo for the San Francisco Conference, at which the United Nations Charter would be drafted and approved. The design of the logo was a circular representation of the map of the world, seen from on top of the North Pole with North America in the center. The General Assembly of the United Nations approved a slightly altered San Francisco design on December 7, 1946. Instead of the USA, the Greenwich Meridian became the emblem's center. Two laurel branches surrounded the map of the world. The olive branch can be traced back to ancient Greece as a symbol of peace. The map of the world symbolized the area in which the United Nations is concerned with achieving peace.

A year later it was felt that there should be a special UN flag. On October 20, 1947, the General Assembly of the United Nations adopted a resolution declaring:

"That the Flag of the United Nations shall be the official emblem adopted by the General Assembly centered on a blue ground."

The United Nations has never given a reason for the choice of light blue as the flag color. It was originally chosen by the then US Secretary of State, Edward R. Stettinius Jr., in February 1945. Since it was first used for the UN flag, light blue has come to be identified as a symbol of peace. Countries such as Palau and the Federated States of Micronesia, whose recent history was influenced by the United Nations, subsequently adopted the light blue. Today, the United Nations has 191 member states (since September 27, 2002).

THE RED CROSS AND RED CRESCENT

The first flag to establish itself as a World Flag was that of the Red Cross Society. It was founded in 1863 in Geneva, Switzerland, to look after the casualties of warfare. It was decided to create a distinctive neutral symbol for hospitals, ambulances, and houses where the wounded were nursed or where there were refugees and relief workers. The Swiss founder, Henri Dunant, proposed the Red Cross flag. He reversed the colors of his own national flag, which is red with a white cross. Switzerland has a long record of neutrality.

As the cross is also the symbol of Christianity, it was acknowledged that not all people might respect the Red Cross as a neutral symbol. In 1876, a special Red Crescent flag was adopted as a sign of neutrality in the Muslim world.

Some other religions use their own symbols, but these are not internationally recognized. Israel, for example, has applied several times for approval of the Red Magen David. Thus far it has failed.

EUROPEAN UNION

The flag of the European Union (EU)—dark blue with a circle of 12 five-pointed yellow stars—was first adopted on December 8, 1955, by the Council of Europe. It repeatedly expressed the desire that other European institutions should adopt the same symbol. Although the European Parliament in Strasbourg, France, expressed the need for an EU flag in 1979, it did not happen until March 1986.

Members of the European Union
(January 1, 2003)

Austria	Italy
Belgium	Luxembourg
Denmark	Netherlands
Finland	Portugal
France	Spain
Germany	Sweden
Greece	United Kingdom
Ireland	

Euro bank notes are now used all over Europe under the EU agreement and depict the European flag.

The flag of the European Union.

Applied for entry
in 2004

Cyprus	Lithuania
Czech Republic	Malta
Estonia	Poland
Hungary	Slovakia
Latvia	Slovenia

Blue signifies the heaven of the west. The 12 stars represent all EU member states; 12 is the representation of perfection. The stars are in a circle, like a round table conference, to symbolize that everyone in Europe is equal.

Non-EU members also use the EU flag as the flag of Europe. In flying the European colors they express the wish to become part of the European family of nations. In some European countries, such as Italy and France, the European flag has to be flown together with the national flag. The current flag of Bosnia and Herzegovina (1998) is modeled on the EU flag, as it suggests neutrality.

NATO—NORTH ATLANTIC TREATY ORGANIZATION

The North Atlantic Treaty Organization (NATO) was established in 1949 as a united defense against the socialist threat, especially Soviet aggression. The signatories promised that they would each support one another if one of them was attacked.

The NATO flag was adopted on October 28, 1953. Its dark blue field represents the Atlantic Ocean. The circle represents unity and the compass showed the common direction toward peace.

The role of the military international organization changed from protection for one another to that of Europe's policeman after the end of the Cold War. NATO has provided support for the United Nations peacekeeping initiatives in several parts of the former Yugoslavia since 1992. Former potential socialist enemies (East Germany, Czech Republic, Poland, and Hungary) were admitted to NATO, after the collapse of communism.

Member states of NATO (year of admission)

(Situation: January 1, 2003)

Belgium (1949)

Canada (1949)

Czech Republic (1999)

Denmark (1949)

France (1949)

Germany (1955)

Greece (1952)

Hungary (1999)

Iceland (1949)

Italy (1949)

Luxembourg (1949)

Netherlands (1949)

Norway (1949)

Poland (1999)

Portugal (1949)

Spain (1982)

Turkey (1952)

United Kingdom (1949)

United States of America (1949)

ORGANIZATION OF AMERICAN STATES

The Organization of American States (OAS) is one of world's oldest international organizations. It was originally established in 1890 for commercial purposes, but was renamed OAS on April 30, 1980. Its aims are to uphold sovereignty and peace in all parts of the American continent.

The OAS flag was adopted in 1965. It has a medium blue field, with a large white disc in its center. The disc holds a trophy of the flags of all member states. When a new member is admitted or a member state alters its flag, the flag of the OAS has to be changed. This has happened regularly since its adoption.

Antigua and
   Barbuda
Argentina
Bahamas
Barbados
Belize
Bolivia
Brazil
Canada
Chile
Colombia
Costa Rica
Cuba
Dominica
Dominican Republic
Ecuador
El Salvador
Grenada
Guatemala
Guyana

Haiti
Honduras
Jamaica
Mexico
Nicaragua
Panama
Paraguay
Peru
St. Kitts-Nevis
St. Lucia
St. Vincent and the
   Grenadines
Surinam
Trinidad and Tobago
Uruguay
United States of
   America
Venezuela

THE COMMONWEALTH

The Commonwealth is an international organization of states which were formerly parts of the United Kingdom or United Nations mandate territories. Currently the Commonwealth has 54 member countries. Its 1.7 billion people make up 30 percent of the world's population. Since it was founded in

Member states of the Commonwealth (year of admission)

(Situation: January 1, 2003)

Antigua and Barbuda (1981)

Australia (1931)

Bahamas (1973)

Bangladesh (1972)

Barbados (1966)

Belize (1981)

Botswana (1966)

Brunei (1984)

Cameroon (1995)

Canada (1931)

Cyprus (1961)

Dominica (1978)

Fiji (1970)

The Gambia (1965)

Ghana (1957)

Grenada (1974)

Guyana (1966)

India (1947)

Jamaica (1962)

Kenya (1963)

Kiribati (1979)

Lesotho (1966)

Malawi (1964)

Malaysia (1957)

Maldives (1982)

Malta (1964)

Mauritius (1968)

Mozambique (1995)

Namibia (1990)

Nauru (1968)

New Zealand (1931)

Nigeria (1960)

Pakistan (1947)

Papua New Guinea (1975)

St. Kitts and Nevis (1983)

St. Lucia (1979)

St. Vincent and the Grenadines (1979)

Samoa (1970)

Seychelles (1976)

Sierra Leone (1961)

Singapore (1965)

Solomon Islands (1978)

South Africa (1931)

Sri Lanka (1948)

Swaziland (1968)

Tanzania (1961)

Tonga (1970)

Trinidad and Tobago (1962)

Tuvalu (1978)

Uganda (1962)

United Kingdom (1931)

Vanuatu (1980)

Zambia (1964)

Zimbabwe (1980)

1931 it has been known as the British Commonwealth, but in 1949 this was changed to the Commonwealth.

The flag is blue, with a graphic representation of the yellow capital letter "C" which stands for Commonwealth. The rays forming the "C" do not represent the number of Commonwealth members. The letter encircles a globe, representing the global scope of the organization.

COMMONWEALTH OF INDEPENDENT STATES (CIS)

The Soviet Union comprised 15 republics, whose economies were linked together and depended heavily on each other. After the disintegration of the Soviet Union in 1991, the Commonwealth of Independent States (CIS) was founded. Twelve of the former 15 Soviet republics have joined so far. The CIS deals

Member states CIS

(Situation: January 1, 2003)

Armenia	Moldova
Azerbaijan	Russia
Belarus	Tajikistan
Georgia	Turkmenistan
Kazakhstan	Ukraine
Kyrgyzstan	Uzbekistan

with matters relating to the break-up of the Soviet Union.

The CIS flag was adopted on January 19, 1996. Its blue field represents peace. The central graphic emblem expresses the will of the member states to cooperate and to form a common house. Its white color signifies purity. The emblem encircles a sun, which is the symbol of light and warmth given to the people.

OLYMPIC GAMES

When the first modern Olympic Games were held in Athens in 1896, no flags were displayed. It took nearly two decades before the Olympic flag was flown for the first time. It was designed by Pierre de Coubertin, the founding father of the modern Olympics in 1913, for display at the 1916 Games. These Games were cancelled however, due to the outbreak of World War I.

The flag was first hoisted in 1920 in Antwerp, Belgium. The first Olympic flag, manufactured by the Magasins du Bon Marché in Paris, is still on display at the Olympic Museum in Lausanne. The white represents the peace and friendship between the competing nations. The five interwoven rings in blue, black, red, yellow, and green represent the five continents. These colors were chosen because they appeared in the flags of all the countries which were independent in 1913. Officially, there are two Olympic flags. One is for display during the Summer Games, the other for use during the Winter Games. The town that organized the last Games is obliged to pass on the flag to the town organizing the next Games.

The Olympic flag waves at the Winter Olympics in 1994.

5 Signaling Flags

Flags have long been used to convey visible messages over a distance. In a way, visual signals were used as early telephones and served to send messages between ships. It has been recorded that during the ancient Greek wars, Themistocles gave the signal to his fleet during one battle to attack the galleys of Xerxes by hoisting a purple cloak. In the Middles Ages, the Venetian and Genoese fleets developed their own signaling systems to pass messages.

Up until the 17th century, flag signals were of an elementary nature. The system was very simple. Every ship had several masts, by flying different flags from different masts, one could "write" at a distance. However, every fleet used its own signals which might also vary from year-to-year, to avoid others deciphering secret messages. This was especially important in wartime, when it was better that the opponent was not able to decode signals with a tactical message.

There were, however, some conventions that were understood internationally. A white flag meant truce and a red flag was the obvious battle signal. The Dutch Wars proved the necessity for ships to have a reliable means of communication. The first printed edition of *Sailing and Fighting Instructions* was published in 1673 by James, Duke of York, Lord High Admiral of Great Britain. It showed how the Admiral of the Fleet could communicate with all of his ships by hoisting flags in different positions. Some of the flags at the start of modern signaling were ordinary standard flags; others were just for signaling.

Various signal codes were tried out. The 1673 Instructions were superseded in 1703 by

Signalmen aboard the USS *George Washington* send messages by flags.

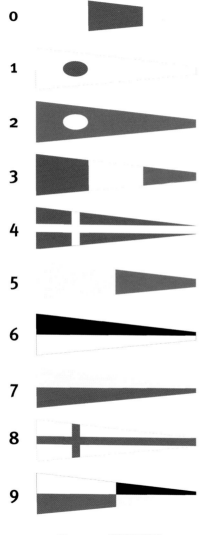

the manual instructions for the *Directing and Governing Her Majesty's Fleet in Sailing and Fighting*. This manual remained in use until 1782. At that time Admiral Lord Howe had published his *Signal Book for the Ships at War*, in which he simplified the range of flags used for signaling. With a lower number of smaller flags, Lord Howe was able to create a greater range of signals. Sir Home Popham developed this system further as a numerical vocabulary. Every number was to be found in the manual. For example the number 53, involving flags 5 and 3, meant "prepare for battle." Number 16 meant "engage the enemy more closely." The only shortcoming of Lord Howe's signal book was that not every word could be given a number.

Until 1817, every merchant shipping company used its own signaling system. At sea these ships were not able to communicate with each other, with one exception. When the national flag or ensign was flown upside down, the ship was in distress. Captain Frederick Marryat of the Royal Navy developed a Code of Signals for the Merchant Service in 1817. This was based on the Howe and Popham principle. At the publication of the 12th edition in 1855 by the Board of Trade, the Code was renamed the *Commercial Code of Signals for Use of all Nations*. It

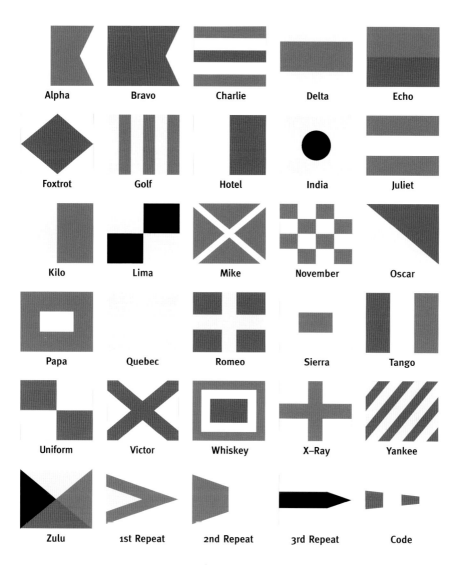

Alpha	Bravo	Charlie	Delta	Echo
Foxtrot	Golf	Hotel	India	Juliet
Kilo	Lima	Mike	November	Oscar
Papa	Quebec	Romeo	Sierra	Tango
Uniform	Victor	Whiskey	X–Ray	Yankee
Zulu	1st Repeat	2nd Repeat	3rd Repeat	Code

contained 70,000 signals and used 18 alphabetical flags.

The Commercial Code was adopted by the principal maritime powers and translated into many languages, becoming the International Code in 1880. This was revised and enlarged by the end of the century to include a separate flag for every letter. It came into use as the *International Code of Signals* on January 1, 1901, and was to be used by the navies of all nations. This first edition, however, did not stand up to the test of the World War I and experience showed that it was not really an international code. The messages were not always clear as some alphabetical flags were rectangular, while others were pennant-shaped. Also, the alphabetical flags sometimes represented numbers.

Great Britain was asked to draft a new signaling code. It took until 1934 for it to come into use. The main improvement was that all alphabetical flags became rectangular and in addition, ten pennants were added to represent the numerals 0 to 9. This code is still in use today. The International Maritime Organization in London adopted the code with some alterations in 1965 and has since been in charge of the publication of the signal book.

Signal flags have lost their importance nowadays as radio, telephone, and the Internet pass messages that were formerly communicated by the signal flags. However, signal flags are still used at festivals to dress ships, when all these flags are flown at "dressing lines." Ships should be dressed only while at anchor or moored in a harbor.

Flags and sails on boats for sale at the US Sailboat Show in Annapolis, Maryland.

Part Two

Gazetteer

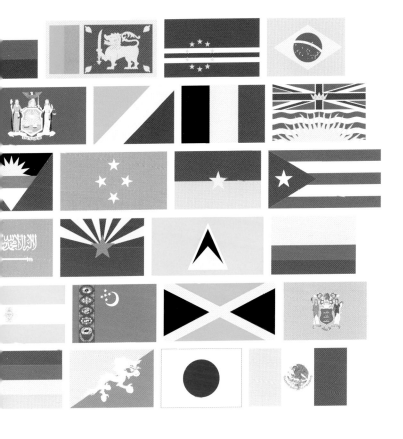

GAZETTEER

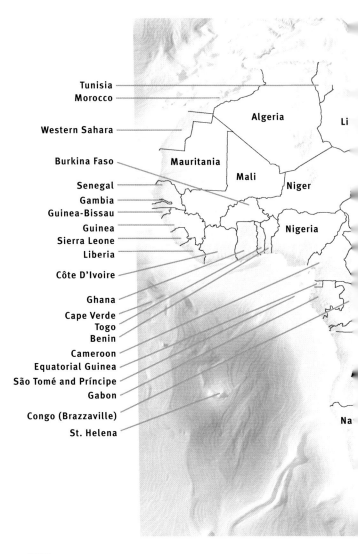

Tunisia

Morocco

Western Sahara

Burkina Faso

Senegal

Gambia

Guinea-Bissau

Guinea

Sierra Leone

Liberia

Côte D'Ivoire

Ghana

Cape Verde

Togo

Benin

Cameroon

Equatorial Guinea

São Tomé and Príncipe

Gabon

Congo (Brazzaville)

St. Helena

Algeria

Li

Mauritania

Mali

Niger

Nigeria

Na

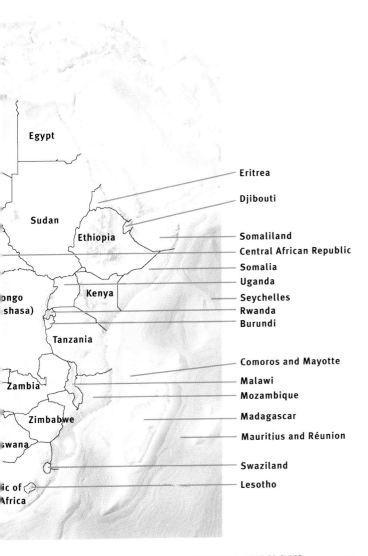

Egypt

Eritrea

Djibouti

Sudan

Ethiopia

Somaliland

Central African Republic

Somalia

Uganda

ongo
shasa)

Kenya

Seychelles

Rwanda

Burundi

Tanzania

Comoros and Mayotte

Zambia

Malawi

Mozambique

Zimbabwe

Madagascar

Mauritius and Réunion

swana

Swaziland

ic of
frica

Lesotho

In terms of nation building, A F R I C A is a young continent. The majority of the 58 African entities achieved independence in the 1960s, but their borders had already been decided with a ruler at the Berlin Conference in 1884–1885, in many cases splitting ancient kingdoms into several parts.

With no flag history, the newborn countries had to design their national flags from scratch. Familiar colors were those of the colonial powers, France, the United Kingdom, Belgium, Spain, and Portugal. In a few cases the new flags were modeled on the former colonial powers but, as most wanted to make a new start, this was done reluctantly. However, many of the new countries admired Ethiopia as it had never been colonized by a European power. They illustrated this by adopting its flag colors of green, yellow, and red. These colors have since become known as the pan-African colors. Yellow often refers to the mineral wealth and green symbolizes the will to become independent from food aid, while red recalls the blood shed in the struggle for independence.

In quite a few cases the party that led the country to independence gave the new nation its flag colors or emblems. This proved to be dangerous; in time most of these parties lost power and were overthrown by new parties who quickly abolished the old political colors. The Comoros, for instance, has had five flags since the country became independent in 1975. In the process of reconciliation in Rwanda, the flag was altered in 2001 in order to remove the emblem under which hundreds of thousands of people were massacred in a bloody civil war.

The United Nations frequently plays an important role in the process of gaining independence and this is reflected in the national flags of Somalia and Eritrea. Somalia uses the same light blue as is used in the United Nations flag, while Eritrea copied the laurel leaves.

Black is a color that is seen very often in African flags. It is always symbolic of the Black Continent, as Africa is known, but it also symbolizes the skin of the African people or a dark history. The stars, which feature on several African flags, often refer to unity or recall (when red) the socialist beliefs of the government.

In the northern part of the African continent, Islam is the predominant religion. This is reflected in the national flags, particularly when green and showing the Islamic star and crescent. Egypt, Sudan, and Western Sahara have adopted the pan-Arab colors and symbols.

Some tiny African territories are still administered from Paris or London. French possessions use the French Tricolore. The British dependency of St. Helena has a miniature version of the Union Flag in the upper canton to show its ties with the United Kingdom.

It is expected that Africa will see new flags in the future; some are seen as overly political and therefore dated. Angola, Mozambique, and Malawi have already announced they will seek new colors in order to reflect their transition into working democracies.

As Africa was divided into nation states on a drawing board, it is to be expected that people might stand up against these divisions and split away. Biafra failed to split from Nigeria in 1967, but Somaliland succeeded in breaking from civil war-torn Somalia in May 1991. It is not yet recognized internationally but has, however, all the means and symbols to act independently. Several other aspirant nations fight for independence and fly their flags in liberated areas.

Algeria

Democratic and Popular Republic of Algeria

After eight years of war against the French, Algeria became independent on July 3, 1962. Its flag was originally designed in 1928 for the independence movement, Front National de Libèration. The green stands for Islam, white for purity, and red for liberty. The star and crescent recall Ottoman rule and the crescent's horns represent prosperity and happiness.

Capital: Algiers
Area (sq. km): 2,381,740
Population: 31,200,000
Languages: Arabic, Berber, English
Currency: Algerian Dinar

Angola

Republic of Angola

This flag is based on that of the independence movement. Red represents the blood shed in the struggle for freedom from Portugal that culminated in independence on November 11, 1975. Black represents Africa, the cogwheel symbolizes the workers, while the machete stands for the peasants. The star indicates international solidarity. The yellow color of the tools reflects the country's wealth.

Capital: Luanda
Area (sq. km): 1,246,700
Population: 10,200,000
Languages: Bantu, Portuguese
Currency: Kwanza

Benin

Republic of Benin

Benin became independent from France on August 1, 1960, as Dahomey and adopted the pan-African colors green, yellow, and red. The colors symbolize nationalism and African unity. After a Marxist revolution in 1975, the name of the country was changed to Benin and a communist star was added to the flag. In 1990, the original flag was restored, but not the old name.

Capital: Porto-Novo
Area (sq. km): 112,600
Population: 6,500,000
Languages: French, Fon, Yurobi
Currency: CFA Franc

Botswana

Republic of Botswana

Life for the people of Botswana is heavily dependent on rain. Their desire for adequate water supply is symbolized in the light blue color. The black stripe edged with white bands expresses the will of the African and European population to live in harmony. The flag was first hoisted on September 30, 1966, when Botswana gained independence from the United Kingdom.

Capital: Gaborone
Area (sq. km): 224,600
Population: 1,600,000
Languages: English, Setswana
Currency: Pula

Burkina Faso

Democratic Republic of Burkina Faso

This country became independent from France on August 5, 1960, as Upper Volta. It adopted a triband flag that symbolized the country's three main rivers which all were named after a color. After a coup d'état the name of the country was changed on August 4, 1984, to Burkina Faso and the flag adopted its current design in the pan-African colors. The yellow star is the guiding light of the revolution.

Capital: Ouagadougou
Area (sq. km): 274,000
Population: 11,000,000
Languages: French, local languages
Currency: CFA Franc

Burundi

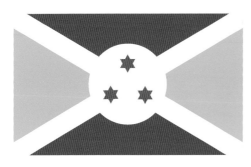

Republic of Burundi

The Burundi flag is based on the flag of the former Belgian air carrier Sabena. Belgium administered Burundi until July 1, 1962, when it became independent. The flag was adopted on June 28, 1967, after a coup d'état. Red is a reminder of the struggle for independence and green stands for hope for a prosperous future. The white cross symbolizes peace between the three main ethnic groups, each represented by a star.

Capital: Bujumbura
Area (sq. km): 27,800
Population: 6,700,000
Languages: French, local languages
Currency: Burundi Franc

Cameroon

Republic of Cameroon

The flag of Cameroon is based on the French flag. France administered the part of Cameroon which first gained independence on January 1, 1960. The pan-African colors represent hope (green), unity (red), and prosperity (yellow). In 1961, British Cameroon joined the former French colony, and was represented by two stars in the flag. These were changed to one single star to represent unity, on May 20, 1975.

Capital: Yaoundé
Area (sq. km): 475,000
Population: 15,450,000
Languages: English, French, local languages
Currency: CFA Franc

Cape Verde

Republic of Cape Verde

Cape Verde is a group of ten islands in the Atlantic Ocean on Africa's northwest coast. Its flag, which was adopted on February 25, 1992, is like a map. Blue represents the Atlantic Ocean, with each island represented by a golden star, in a circle symbolizing equality. The red stripe between the white symbolizes the road of progress. Cape Verde became independent from Portugal on July 5, 1975.

Capital: Praia
Area (sq. km): 4,000
Population: 400,000
Languages: Creole, Portuguese
Currency: Escudo Caboverdiano

Central African Republic

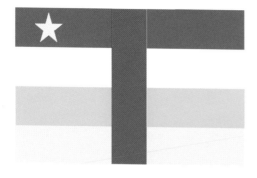

Central African Republic

The Central African Republic combines in its flag the French and pan-African colors. The French colors symbolize the former colonial ruler, which led the country to independence on August 13, 1960. The Central African Republic hoped that other French colonies would join a federation. The yellow star represents that hope; the goal, however, has not been achieved.

Capital: Bangui
Area (sq. km): 623,000
Population: 3,500,000
Languages: French, indigenous languages
Currency: CFA Franc

Chad

Republic of Chad

The flag of Chad is identical to that of Romania. When Chad became independent from France on August 11, 1960, it honored its former colonial power by copying the French Tricolore. It changed the central band to yellow, creating a flag in pan-African colors. Yellow represents the sun and desert, blue the sky and water, while red symbolizes progress.

Capital: N'Djamena
Area (sq. km): 1,284,000
Population: 7,500,000
Languages: Arabic, French, Sara, indigenous
Currency: CFA Franc

Comoros

Union of the Comoros

The Comoros is a group of four islands in the Indian Ocean on Africa's east coast. When they became independent on July 6, 1975, the island of Mayotte stayed with France. This island is still represented in the flag adopted on December 23, 2001. Each of the four bands, as well as each star, represents one of the islands. The crescent on the green triangle symbolizes the Islamic faith.

Capital: Moroni
Area (sq. km): 2,235
Population: 550,000
Languages: Comoran, French, Arabic
Currency: Comorian Franc

Congo (Brazzaville)

Republic of the Congo

Congo (Brazzaville) adopted a flag in the pan-African colors when it gained independence from France on August 15, 1960. As this combination of colors was used in many variations by other African countries, Congo arranged them diagonally. Between 1970 and June 4, 1991, it used a different national flag. Green represents nature, yellow is natural wealth, and red symbolizes human blood.

Capital: Brazzaville
Area (sq. km): 342,000
Population: 2,900,000
Languages: French, Lingale, Kikongo
Currency: CFA Franc

Congo (Kinshasa)

Democratic Republic of the Congo

Between 1971 and May 17, 1997, this former Belgian colony was known as Zaire. The flag adopted at independence on June 30, 1960, was not used between 1963 and May 1997. The flag is based on the flag of the Congo Free State, which was blue with a big yellow star. The six stars at the hoist represent the original six provinces of the vast country.

Capital: Kinshasa
Area (sq. km): 2,345,000
Population: 52,500,000
Languages: French, 400 local languages
Currency: Congolese Franc

Côte D'Ivoire

Republic of Côte d'Ivoire

It is forbidden by law to translate the country's name into Ivory Coast. The country became independent from France on August 7, 1960, and adopted a flag modeled on the French Tricolore which resembles the Irish flag. Orange represents the savannah grassland, white the rivers, and green the forests to be found at the coast.

Capital: Yamoussoukro
Area (sq. km): 322,500
Population: 16,000,000
Languages: French, indigenous
Currency: CFA Franc

Djibouti

Republic of Djibouti

The flag of Djibouti is modeled on that of
the party that led the country to
independence from France on June 27,
1977. The two major ethnic people of
the country are the Afar and Issa. Light
blue represents the Issa and green the
Afar. The triangle recalls the words in
the national motto: Unity, Equality,
Peace; white represents peace, and the
red star stands for unity.

Capital: Djibouti
Area (sq. km): 23,200
Population: 452,000
Languages: French, indigenous
Currency: Djibouti Franc

Egypt

Arab Republic of Egypt

When Egypt became independent as a
kingdom on February 28, 1922, it
adopted a green flag with crescents to
recall Islam. In 1952, the country
became a republic and adopted the
pan-Arab colors red, white, and black.
Egypt became part of the Federation of
Arab Republics with Syria and Libya in
1972 under the same pan-Arab flag. This
lasted until 1977. The eagle of Saladin
was introduced on October 4, 1984.

Capital: Cairo
Area (sq. km): 1,001,500
Population: 69,000,000
Languages: Arabic
Currency: Egyptian Pound

Equatorial Guinea

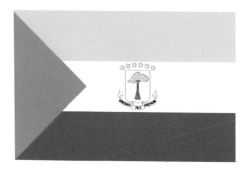

Republic of Equatorial Guinea

The flag of the former Spanish colony of Equatorial Guinea was first hoisted on Independence Day, October 12, 1968. The blue triangle symbolizes the Atlantic Ocean. The agricultural lands are reflected by the green stripe, the white stripe reflects peace, and the red stripe stands for independence. In the center of the flag the arms of the country are depicted. It contains six stars for the six parts of the state.

Capital: Malabo
Area (sq. km): 28,000
Population: 475,000
Languages: Spanish, French, Ibo
Currency: CFA Franc

Eritrea

State of Eritrea

Eritrea became independent on May 24, 1993, after a long war against Ethiopia. Its flag is a combination of that of the Eritrean People's Liberation Front (EPLF) and the olive branch of the United Nations flag. The EPLF led the struggle for independence and the UN granted Eritrea autonomy. Green represents agriculture, red the struggle for independence, blue the marine wealth, and yellow the mineral wealth.

Capital: Asmara
Area (sq. km): 124.300
Population: 3,600,000
Languages: Arabic, Tigrinya, English
Currency: Nakfa

Ethiopia

Federal Democratic Republic of Ethiopia

Ethiopia gave many African countries the colors of their flags. The country put the three traditional colors green, yellow, and red together to form a flag in 1895. As tribute to the pure African roots of Ethiopia, other African nations adopted the same colors. In 1996, the blue disc with the golden star was added to the Ethiopian flag; blue stands for peace and the star for unity.

Capital: Addis Ababa
Area (sq. km): 1,104,300
Population: 63,500,000
Languages: Amharic, 70 local languages
Currency: Ethiopian Birr

Gabon

Gabonese Republic

When Gabon became independent from France on August 17, 1960, it hoisted the green-yellow-blue flag. This color combination, which is unique for Africa, was adopted several days before the flag raising. The "light Irish green" represents the tropical forest. The golden yellow band is the symbol for the sun. The royal blue band symbolizes the Atlantic Ocean.

Capital: Librevllle
Area (sq. km): 267,700
Population: 1,210,000
Languages: French, Fang
Currency: CFA Franc

Gambia

Republic of The Gambia

The Gambian flag adopted on February 18, 1965, when the country became independent from the United Kingdom, does not have a political basis. The blue stripe between the small white stripes symbolizes the River Gambia, after which the country is named, and its banks where the people live. North of the river is the savannah, symbolized by the red band. South is the tropical forest recalled by the green band.

Capital: Banjul
Area (sq. km): 11,300
Population: 1,300,000
Languages: English, Fula, Jola
Currency: Dalasi

Ghana

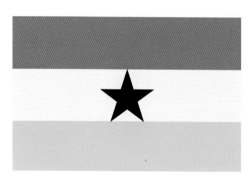

Republic of Ghana

Ghana (formerly Gold Coast) was the first African country to become independent from colonial rule, on March 6, 1957. As a salute to Ethiopia, it adopted the same flag colors. Red commemorates the struggle for independence, gold represents the mineral wealth of the country, green is for the forests and farms, and the black star symbolizes African freedom.

Capital: Accra
Area (sq. km): 238,600
Population: 19,000,000
Languages: English, Twi, Fanti
Currency: Cedi

Guinea

Republic of Guinea

The flag of Guinea, introduced on Independence Day October 2, 1958, is modeled on the Tricolore of the colonial power France. It adopted the pan-African colors red, yellow, and green, introduced by Ghana in its flag a year earlier. Red symbolizes the struggle for independence. Yellow recalls the sun and the mineral wealth. Green represents the forests of the country.

Capital: Conakry
Area (sq. km): 246,000
Population: 7,500,000
Languages: French, Soussou, Fullah
Currency: Guinea Franc

Guinea-Bissau

Republic of Guinea-Bissau

Guinea-Bissau adopted the pan-African colors when it split away from Portugal on September 24, 1973 (who only recognized this a year later). The flag is modeled on the flag of the leading independence party. Red stands for the blood shed in the war against the colonial power. Yellow represents the sun and green is for hope in a better future. The black star symbolizes African unity.

Capital: Bissau
Area (sq. km): 36,150
Population: 1,300,000
Languages: Portuguese, Creole
Currency: CFA Franc

Kenya

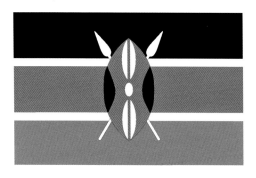

Republic of Kenya

At the time of Kenyan independence on December 12, 1963, the ruling party was the Kenya Africa National Union (KANU), and the national flag looks very similar to the KANU flag. To create the national flag the white fimbriations, symbolizing democracy, were added to the dark red stripe and the spears and shield (representing the defense of the country) were redrawn.

Capital: Nairobi
Area (sq. km): 582,700
Population: 31,000,000
Languages: Swahili, English
Currency: Kenya Shilling

Lesotho

Kingdom of Lesotho

The flag Lesotho adopted at independence on October 4, 1966, was based on colors of the leading party. After a coup d'état in 1986 the national flag was changed to a non-political design. The national motto is "Khotso-Pula-Nala," meaning Peace, Rain, and Plenty, symbolized by the colors white, blue, and green respectively. The African design shield contains a crocodile, to recall King Moshoeshoe, the first king.

Capital: Maseru
Area (sq. km): 30,400
Population: 2,200,000
Languages: Sesotho, English
Currency: Loti

Liberia

Republic of Liberia

Liberia, literally, means freedom. The country was established on July 26, 1847, for free slaves in the United States. The flag, adopted on the same day, is modeled on the Stars and Stripes. The 11 red and white stripes represent the 11 states that agreed on the founding of Liberia. The blue canton symbolizes Africa, and the white star represents the light that would shine on African freedom.

Capital: Monrovia
Area (sq. km): 97,800
Population: 3,200,000
Languages: English, Bassa, Kru
Currency: Liberian Dollar

Libya

Great Socialist People's Libyan Arab Jamahiriya

Libya achieved independence from Italy on December 24, 1951, and is the only country in the world with a flag of a single plain color. The dark green flag was adopted in 1977 to represent both Islam and the Green Revolution. President Gadaffi wished his country to become green with crops, so as to be independent of foreign food.

Capital: Tripoli
Area (sq. km): 1,760,000
Population: 5,200,000
Languages: Arabic, Berber
Currency: Libyan Dinar

Madagascar

Republic of Madagascar

Before the French made a colony of Madagascar, the island was the Hova Kingdom, built up from several previous kingdoms. The Hova Kingdom used a flag of white, red, and green—adopted as the national colors of Madagascar, which achieved independence on June 26, 1960. White represents purity, red independence, and green symbolizes hope.

Capital: Antananarivo
Area (sq. km): 587,000
Population: 15,700,000
Languages: French, English, Malagasy
Currency: Franc Malgache

Malawi

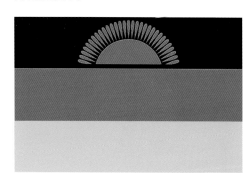

Republic of Malawi

The flag of Malawi is that of the Malawi Congress Party, enhanced with a sun. Malawi was granted independence from the United Kingdom on July 6, 1964. The red sun (called kwacha) with its 31 red rays is more than a flag symbol. The name Malawi means "flaming waters," and refers to the color of the sun when mirrored in Lake Nyasa; it also symbolizes the new dawn for the country.

Capital: Lilongwe
Area (sq. km): 118,500
Population: 10,500,000
Languages: Chichewa, English
Currency: Kwacha

Mali

Republic of Mali

Mali together with Senegal achieved independence from France on June 20, 1960, but the federation split by September 22, the same year. Mali kept the flag the federation used, but omitted the kanaga (man) emblem in the central stripe. The Mali flag is modeled on the French Tricolore. Green symbolizes agricultural resources, yellow purity, and red the struggle for independence.

Capital: Bamako
Area (sq. km): 1,240,200
Population: 10,750,000
Languages: French, Bambara, Senufo
Currency: CFA Franc

Mauritania

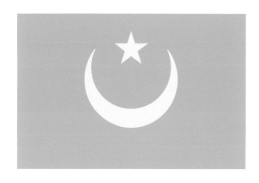

Republic of Mauritania

The Mauritanian flag shows in all its aspects that the country is Islamic. Green represents the hope for a better future. The moon and star represent Islam as well. The crescent moon symbolizes the people's will to become mature. The yellow color refers to the endless sand views of the Sahara Desert.

Capital: Nouakchott
Area (sq. km): 1,030,700
Population: 2,300,000
Languages: Arabic, French, Pular
Currency: Ouguiya

Mauritius

Republic of Mauritius

The island of Mauritius, in the Indian Ocean, is named after the Dutch prince Maurits of Nassau. It achieved independence from the United Kingdom on March 12, 1968. As the country didn't have ideas for a flag, the College of Arms in London was asked to design the national flag. It transferred the colors used in the coat of arms (granted in 1906) as stripes on the flag.

Capital: Port Louis
Area (sq. km): 2,040
Population: 1,200,000
Languages: English, French, Creole, Hindi
Currency: Mauritius Rupee

Mayotte

Territorial Collectivity of Mayotte

The island of Mayotte is part of the Comoros archipelago. When Comoros became independent in 1975, Mayotte decided to stay with France for economic reasons. It has the status of Territorial Collectivity and therefore uses the French Tricolore as the national flag. The Comoros didn't accept Mayotte's decision to stay French and symbolizes Mayotte in its own flag.

Capital: Mamoudzou
Area (sq. km): 375
Population: 140,000
Languages: French, Arabic
Currency: Euro

Morocco

Kingdom of Morocco

Although Morocco achieved independence from France on March 2, 1956, its flag dates back to November 17, 1915, when the green star was added to the plain red flag. Red is said to denote the blood ties between the rulers of Morocco and the Prophet Muhammad. The green star—an interlaced pentangle —represents the Seal of Solomon which was used as a law symbol for centuries.

Capital: Rabat
Area (sq. km): 446,500
Population: 30,600,000
Languages: Arabic, Berber, French, Spanish
Currency: Dirham

Mozambique

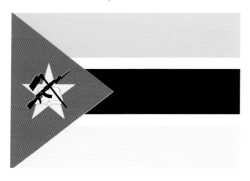

Republic of Mozambique

Frelimo, the party that led Mozambique to independence from Portugal on June 25, 1975, gave the national flag its basis. The current flag however was adopted May 1, 1983, to celebrate the fact that the country had become a one party state. Red recalls the bloody war for independence. It is expected that Mozambique will adopt a new flag in due course, to symbolize the multiparty system the country embraced in 1994.

Capital: Maputo
Area (sq. km): 799,4000
Population: 19,200,000
Languages: Portuguese, Bantu, Swahili
Currency: Metical

Namibia

Republic of Namibia

Namibia was one of the African countries to achieve independence most recently on March 21, 1990. It had been administered by neighboring South Africa since 1920. The flag was the winning design from 835 entries submitted by the public. It combined the colors of SWAPO and the Democratic Turnhalle Alliance, the major political parties at the time of independence. The sun represents life and energy.

Capital: Windhoek
Area (sq. km): 824,300
Population: 1,800,000
Languages: English, German, Afrikaans
Currency: Namibian Dollar

Niger

Republic of Niger

Niger is situated mainly in the Sahara Desert. The orange band recalls the geographical situation of the country, which became independent from France on August 3, 1960. At that time there was a strong sentiment to merge with neighboring Côte d'Ivoire, whose flag colors are the same. The orange disc represents the sun, white stands for purity, and green for the country's grasslands. Niger's flag is similar to that of India.

Capital: Niamey
Area (sq. km): 1,267,000
Population: 10,100,000
Languages: French, Hausa, Djerma
Currency: CFA Franc

Nigeria

Federal Republic of Nigeria

When flying over his country on his way to London, the Nigerian student M. Akinkoenmi was stunned by how green it was. Seeing the vast forests inspired him when he drew his entry for the competition for a national flag design. The flag was first flown when Nigeria became independent from the United Kingdom on October 1, 1960. The white central stripe is meant to symbolize peace and unity.

Capital: Lagos
Area (sq. km): 923,800
Population: 125,000,000
Languages: English, Ibo, 500 indigenous languages
Currency: Naira

Réunion

Department of Réunion

The island of Réunion in the Indian Ocean is in fact part of France. It became a French possession in 1638 and a French department in 1946. Therefore, Réunion's flag is the French Tricolore. Moves to establish a local flag for the island has failed so far. In 2002, Réunion was the first country to use the euro officially.

Capital: St. Denis (Paris)
Area (sq. km): 2,500
Population: 725,000
Languages: French
Currency: Euro

Rwanda

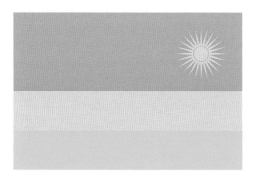

Rwandese Republic

Since independence from Belgium on July 1, 1962, Rwanda has been divided by the Hutu and Tutsi people. Over a period of 30 years, the civil war culminated in genocide in 1994, when 800,000 people were massacred. As a result of the peace process, Rwanda adopted its current flag on December 31, 2001. Green symbolizes hope for prosperity, yellow wealth, and blue peace. The sun stands for the light that guides all people.

Capital: Kigali
Area (sq. km): 26,400
Population: 8,500,000
Languages: French, English, Swahili
Currency: Rwanda Franc

St. Helena

St. Helena and Dependencies

The island of St. Helena in the Atlantic Ocean is a British Dependency, which is obvious by its flag. It is a blue ensign with the island's arms in the fly. These were given to St. Helena by Queen Elizabeth II on October 4, 1985. The ship is a reminder that the East India Company annexed the island in 1659. The bird is the endemic wirebird. This flag is also flown in the neighboring islands Tristan da Cunha and Ascension.

Capital: Jamestown
Area (sq. km): 122
Population: 6,500
Languages: English
Currency: St. Helena Pound

São Tomé and Príncipe

Democratic Republic of São Tomé and Príncipe

The independence party, MLSTP, designed the flag of the island republic of São Tomé and Príncipe. Portugal had granted the islands' independence on July 12, 1975. The flag, using the pan-African colors, was adopted by the parliament on November 5, 1975. The two stars represent the two islands. Black recalls the African inhabitants. The red triangle recalls the victims of the struggle for independence.

Capital: São Tomé
Area (sq. km): 1,000
Population: 130,000
Languages: Portuguese
Currency: Dobra

Senegal

Republic of Senegal

Senegal's flag differs from that of neighboring Mali only by its green star. The similarity originates from 1960 when both countries briefly formed the Mali Federation when it gained independence from France. That flag, made up from the pan-African colors, had a black kanaga (man) symbol in the central stripe. After Senegal pulled out of the federation it was replaced by the star to represent unity.

Capital: Dakar
Area (sq. km): 197,000
Population: 10,000,000
Languages: French, many local languages
Currency: CFA Franc

Seychelles

Republic of Seychelles

The island republic of Seychelles adopted its current flag on June 18, 1996. Since independence from the United Kingdom on June 28, 1976, it has had several flags; the current one is non-political in origin. Blue represents the sky and the sea, yellow the sun which gives life and light, red is for unity, white justice, and green the land and natural environment.

Capital: Victoria
Area (sq. km): 455
Population: 80,000
Languages: English, French, Creole
Currency: Seychelles Rupee

Sierra Leone

Republic of Sierra Leone

The flag of Sierra Leone was first hoisted on April 27, 1960, when the former British colony became independent. The tricolor was a result of a design competition. The green stripe represents Sierra Leone's agriculture, natural resources, and her mountains. White stands for unity and justice. Blue signifies the hope that Sierra Leone's unique natural harbor may make its contribution to world peace.

Capital: Freetown
Area (sq. km): 71,750
Population: 5,200,000
Languages: Creole, English
Currency: Leone

Somalia

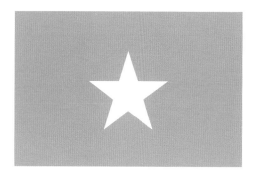

Somali Republic

The United Nations played an important role in the history of Somalia, which is expressed by the adoption of UN blue. Somalia achieved independence on July 1, 1960 when the former British Somaliland also joined. The white star with five points represents unity of the five territories. It expresses the hope that Djibouti, the Ogaden in Ethiopia, and Northern Kenya, will also join Somalia.

Capital: Mogadishu
Area (sq. km): 637,700
Population: 7,300,000
Languages: Arabic, English, Italian, Berber
Currency: Somali Shilling

Somaliland

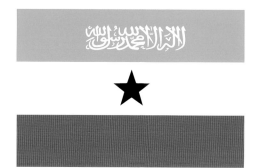

Republic of Somaliland

The former British Somaliland joined Somalia in 1960. As Somaliland it broke away from the civil war torn country on May 18, 1991. The country acts as an independent state but is not recognized as such by the rest of the world. The flag was adopted on October 14, 1996. The green top stripe, representing Islam, has the Arabic inscription: "There is no God but Allah and Muhammad is his Prophet," and the star stands for unity.

Capital: Hargeisa
Area (sq. km): 109,000
Population: 1,500,000
Languages: English, Arabic
Currency: Somaliland Shilling

South Africa

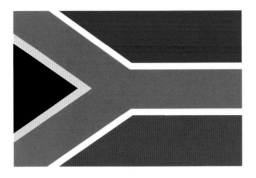

Republic of South Africa

South Africa abandoned its apartheid system on April 27, 1994. The orange, white, and blue flag, which has come to represent white superiority was abolished. A new flag, designed by the chief Herald of South Africa during a flag congress in 1993, expresses that people coming from different directions will follow the same future path (the horizontal "Y"). Black, green, and yellow represent the black majority; red, white, and blue represent the whites.

Capital: Pretoria
Area (sq. km): 1,220,000
Population: 43,500,000
Languages: English, Afrikaans, Zulu, Xhosa
Currency: Rand

Sudan

Republic of Sudan

Sudan's flag was introduced May 20, 1970. It was designed by Abdelrahman Ahmed Aljali, a student at the Art Academy of Khartoum. The flag, in the pan-Arabic colors, superseded the one which had been flown since independence on New Year's Day, 1956. Red symbolizes the blood shed for freedom, and white recalls Islam, peace, light, and love. Black stands for revolution, and green for prosperity and agriculture.

Capital: Khartoum
Area (sq. km): 2,506,000
Population: 35,200,000
Languages: Arabic, English, indigenous languages
Currency: Sudanese Dinar

Swaziland

Kingdom of Swaziland

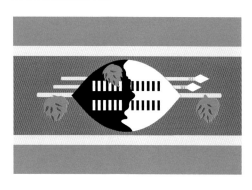

When Swaziland became independent from the United Kingdom on September 6, 1968, it already had its flag. Designed by Emily Shongwe, a relative of the King, it shows a black and white Swazi shield of the Emasotsha Regiment. The shield is decorated with the royal feathers of the widowbird. Crimson stands for the battles in the past, yellow represents mineral wealth, and blue signifies peace.

Capital: Mbabane
Area (sq. km): 17,400
Population: 1,100,000
Languages: English, Swazi
Currency: Lilangeni

Tanzania

United Republic of Tanzania

Tanzania is made up of two countries. Tanganyika, on the African mainland, and the islands of Zanzibar and Pemba on the east coast, united on April 27, 1964, but a common flag had to wait until the end of June that same year. Black represents the people, green the land, blue is said to represent the adjoining sea, and the yellow fimbriation of the black diagonal bar recalls the mineral wealth of the country.

Capital: Dar es Salaam
Area (sq. km): 945,100
Population: 32,000,000
Languages: Kisuaheli, English
Currency: Tanzanian Shilling

Togo

Togolese Republic

Togo's flag was first hoisted on independence from France on April 27, 1960. It is made up from the pan-African colors. Green symbolizes the green revolution and the will to feed all the people. Yellow represents the belief that Togo will develop in all possible ways and red recalls the blood shed by the country's heroes. The white star symbolizes the light and victory. The five stripes recall the five regions of Togo.

Capital: Lomé
Area (sq. km): 56,800
Population: 5,100,000
Languages: French, indigenous languages
Currency: CFA Franc

Tunisia

Republic of Tunisia

The flag of Tunisia is very similar to the Turkish national flag. For a long time Tunisia was part of the Ottoman Empire. Its flag was introduced somewhere around 1835, and was long seen in the Western world as a pirate flag. Between 1881 and March 20, 1956, Tunisia was French. At independence the old flag was reintroduced. The red crescent and star represent Islam, the country's main religion.

Capital: Tunis
Area (sq. km): 163,100
Population: 9,600,000
Languages: Arabic, French
Currency: Tunisian Dinar

Uganda

Republic of Uganda

Uganda introduced its flag on October 9, 1962, on independence from the United Kingdom. It shows the national emblem, a crested crane, on a white disc on six horizontal black, yellow, and red stripes. These were the party colors of the ruling UPC party. Black symbolizes Africa and the color of the skin of the people, yellow is the sunshine, red that everyone's blood is red and the brotherhood of man.

Capital: Kampala
Area (sq. km): 141,200
Population: 23,350,000
Languages: Kisuaheli, English
Currency: Uganda Shilling

Western Sahara

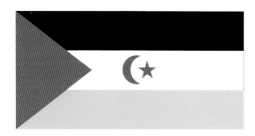

Democratic Sahrawi Arab Republic

Western Sahara, a former Spanish possession, is occupied by Morocco because of its mineral wealth. Most Sahrawi live in refugee camps in Algeria, where the government of the Western Sahara is also based. Western Sahara was declared independent on February 27, 1976, by the Polisario movement. Its flag is modeled on the pan-Arab colors introduced in 1916. The crescent and star symbolize Islam.

Capital: El aaiun / Laâyoune
Area (sq. km): 252,100
Population: 210,000
Languages: Arab
Currency: Moroccan Dirham

Zambia

Republic of Zambia

The flag of Zambia was hoisted for the first time at midnight on October 23, 1964, when the country became independent from the United Kingdom. Green represents the beautiful, red the blood shed during the struggle for independence, black the people of the country, and orange the copper found in Zambia. The eagle in flight represents freedom and the ability to rise above the country's problems.

Capital: Lusaka
Area (sq. km): 752,600
Population: 9,600,000
Languages: English, Bantu
Currency: Kwacha

Zimbabwe

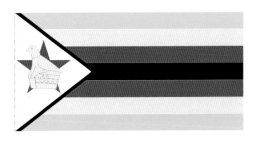

Republic of Zimbabwe

Until Zimbabwe became independent on April 18, 1980, and when the flag was first hoisted, the country was known as Rhodesia. Black represents the black majority while red recalls the armed struggle for independence. Yellow stands for mineral wealth and green for vegetation. The white triangle represents the will for peace and the red star the nation's aspirations. The bird is a symbol found in the ancient city of Zimbabwe after which the country is named.

Capital: Harare
Area (sq. km): 390,750
Population: 11,400,000
Languages: English, Shona, Ndebele
Currency: Zimbabwe Dollar

Children wave the British and Ghana flags during a visit by Queen Elizabeth II to Ghana.

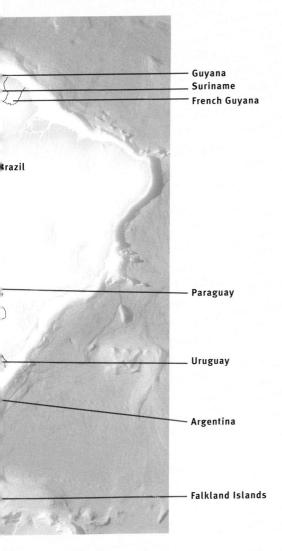

Guyana
Suriname
French Guyana

Brazil

Paraguay

Uruguay

Argentina

Falkland Islands

SOUTH AMERICA is mainly divided into Spanish and Portuguese speaking areas. However, in a few places other languages are spoken, such as Dutch, English, and French, revealing former colonial powers. Two of the 14 South American countries are still owned by a European power, which is reflected in their flags.

From the beginning of the 16th century, the Spanish and Portuguese were mainly interested in the mineral wealth of South America. Here they found gold and silver in abundance, but in addition to chasing noble metals, they converted indigenous Indians to Catholicism. Those Europeans who settled in South America soon mixed with the indigenous people and, slowly but surely, were alienated from their mother country.

The independence of the United States of America in 1776 fueled the first South American demands for autonomy and independence. The annexation of Portugal and Spain by Napoleon at the beginning of the 19th century further stimulated this desire.

Francisco de Miranda hoisted the first modern South American flag on August 4, 1806. Fighting for an independent Venezuela, he experimented with several designs before he devised a yellow, blue, and red tricolor. By using these colors De Miranda symbolized that the golden South America (yellow) is separated by the Atlantic Ocean (blue) from the hated Spanish tyrants (red). Although De Miranda failed, Venezuela achieved independence a couple of years later on July 5, 1811, and the same colors were adopted in the national flag. The width of the yellow stripe was doubled to express that the golden South America was free.

Venezuela's independence was the sign for the neighboring countries to take up weapons against the Spanish. They were helped by General Simon Bolívar, whose aim it was to establish a united South America. On December 17, 1819, Bolívar declared the Republic of Greater Colombia, which, apart from Venezuela also included Colombia and Ecuador. This union adopted De Miranda's yellow, blue, and red tricolor. The union was brief and dissolved into three independent countries in 1830. All three states recall their common history in their national flag; nowadays they all make use of the colors and pattern introduced by De Miranda. Peru and Bolivia were also liberated with the help of General Simon Bolívar, but never adopted De Miranda's colors.

Argentina and Uruguay use flags of the same colors and the same emblems. The colors were introduced on May 25, 1810—the day the insurrection against the Spanish began in Buenos Aires—inspired by a break in the clouds through which the sun started shining. Blue and white symbolize the breaking of the clouds, while the sun (known as "The Sun of May") looks to a happy future for the country. Uruguay was a province of Argentina when it started revolting against Spain, but decided to go its own way. It adopted a flag modeled on the U.S. Stars and Stripes but used Argentina's colors and the "Sun of May" emblem.

The American flag was also used as a model for the flag of Chile. An American artist, who fought with the Chileans against the Spanish, designed it. The red, white, and blue featuring in the Chilean flag were also used in the Paraguay flag; however this is modeled on the French Tricolore.

Brazil was initially a Portuguese colony, before becoming a separate Portuguese kingdom in 1815. All ties with Portugal were cut in 1822 and Brazil was declared independent. The new country was an empire until 1889, and adopted green and yellow as its national colors. The colors recall the agricultural and mineral wealth of the country.

North of Brazil are situated the three Guyanas. Two of them became independent in the second half of 20th century and adopted newly created national flags. French Guyana, the last remaining colony on the South American mainland, uses the French flag, in order to express the ties with the European mother country. The Falklands and South Georgia islands are British dependencies and fly flags based on the Union Flag.

Argentina

Argentine Republic

It was cloudy in Buenos Aires on May 25, 1810, when the first liberation rally against the Spanish started. During the gathering, the white clouds parted to reveal the shining golden sun in a blue sky. This weather change was seen as a good omen. It is recalled in the Argentine flag, which was created by Manuel Belgrano, the leader of the uprising at the Battle of Rosario in 1812. Independence was achieved on July 9, 1816.

Capital: Buenos Aires
Area (sq. km): 2,766,900
Population: 37,200,000
Languages: Spanish
Currency: Peso

Bolivia

Republic of Bolivia

Simon Bolívar achieved independence from Spain on August 6, 1825, and his country was named after him. Red, yellow, and green were adopted as state colors the next year and altered on November 30, 1851, into their current order. Red symbolizes the valor shown during the struggle for independence, yellow the country's mineral wealth, and green the fertility of the land.

Capital: La Paz
Area (sq km): 1,098,600
Population: 8,250,000
Languages: Spanish
Currency: Boliviano

Brazil

Federative Republic of Brazil

The globe in the Brazilian flag shows 27 stars, each representing one of the states of the Federative Republic. It shows the cloudless sky over Rio de Janeiro on November 15, 1889, when the republic was promulgated and the flag was adopted. Brazil had already obtained its independence from Portugal in 1822. Green symbolizes the Brazilian rainforests. The yellow diamond recalls the mineral wealth of the country.

Capital: Brasilia
Area (sq. km): 8,512,000
Population: 170,000,000
Languages: Portuguese, Indian languages
Currency: Real

Chile

Republic of Chile

The Chilean flag is modeled on the American Stars and Stripes. Charles Wood, an American artist, who fought with the Chilean freedom fighters, designed it. The flag was first displayed on October 18, 1817, a few months before independence from Spain. The Andean skies are represented by the blue canton. The star is for unity, red recalls the blood shed in the struggle for freedom. White is the snow in the Andes.

Capital: Santiago
Area (sq. km): 756,650
Population: 15,200,000
Languages: Spanish
Currency: Chilean Peso

Colombia

Republic of Colombia

The flags of Colombia, and its neighboring states, Ecuador and Venezuela, not only look very similar but they also have a common history. The three countries became independent from Spain as Greater Colombia in 1819, under liberation leader Francisco de Miranda. The federation split on May 30, 1830. Colombia retained the flag used by Greater Colombia and which were originally De Miranda's colors.

Capital: Bogotá
Area (sq. km): 1,138,900
Population: 41,000,000
Languages: Spanish
Currency: Colombian Peso

Ecuador

Republic of Ecuador

In 1822 Ecuador joined the federation of Greater Colombia, set up by De Miranda in 1819. On May 13, 1830, Ecuador seceded the federation, but retained the flag used by Greater Colombia, like its neighbor, Colombia. However, to distinguish its flag, Ecuador has included the national arms in the center.

Capital: Quito
Area (sq. km): 283,750
Population: 12,500,000
Languages: Spanish, Quechua
Currency: US Dollar

Falkland Islands

Falkland Islands

The Falkland Islands are a British Dependent Territory, which is expressed in the flag. It is a British blue ensign, charged in the fly with the coat of arms of the territory. The flag was first hoisted in the islands on September 29, 1948, when the current arms received Royal approval. The arms show a ram evoking the economy's dependence on sheep. The ship is the *Desire* of Captain Davis, who first sighted the Falklands in 1592.

Capital: Stanley
Area (sq. km): 12,200
Population: 2,400
Languages: English
Currency: Falkland Pound

French Guyana

Department of French Guyana

Since 1946, French Guyana has had the same status as the departments on the European mainland. It flies the French blue, white, and red Tricolore as its national flag but occasionally another flag is seen which show the colors of the small independence movement. French Guyana is the last remaining colony on the South American mainland.

Capital: Cayenne
Area (sq. km): 83,500
Population: 159,000
Languages: French
Currency: Euro

Guyana

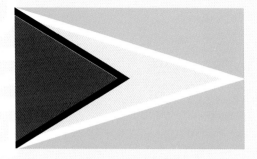

Cooperative Republic of Guyana

The Constitution of Guyana came into force on independence from the UK on May 26, 1966. It states that the national flag is called "The Golden Arrowhead." It was designed by the American flag expert Whitney Smith. The yellow and green stand for the country's mineral and agricultural resources. The golden arrow symbolizes the bright future. Red stands for the zeal and dynamism in building the nation.

Capital: Georgetown
Area (sq. km): 215,000
Population: 700,000
Languages: English, Hindi, Urdu
Currency: Guyana Dollar

Paraguay

Republic of Paraguay

The French national flag became a symbol of freedom and liberation at the beginning of the 19th century. Paraguay declared independence from Spain on May 14, 1811. The country copied the French colors and arranged them horizontally. The flag in its current form was adopted on November 25, 1842, when the arms showing "The Star of May" were added. The reverse of the flag is charged with the Treasury Seal.

Capital: Asunción
Area (sq. km): 406,750
Population: 5,600,000
Languages: Spanish, Guarani
Currency: Guarani

Peru

Republic of Peru

It is said that while fighting the Spaniards in 1820, the liberation leader José de San Martín found the idea for the Peruvian flag when he looked in the sky and saw a flock of flamingos: the red and white colors fascinated him. It is more likely the flag colors were derived from the Inca Empire which ruled Peru before the Spanish. Independence was declared on July 28, 1821. The flag was approved on February 25, 1825. The state flag is charged with the national arms

Capital: Lima
Area (sq. km): 1,285,200
Population: 27,100,000
Languages: Spanish, Quechua, Aymar
Currency: New Sol

Suriname

Republic of Suriname

Suriname's flag was first hoisted on November 25, 1975, when the former Dutch Guyana obtained independence. Green represents the fertility of the country and stands for hope in a prosperous future for the new Suriname. White symbolizes justice and also represents freedom. Red recalls progressiveness. The central star symbolizes the unity of the nation; its yellow color represents sacrifice.

Capital: Paramaribo
Area (sq. km): 163,250
Population: 432,000
Languages: Dutch, Spanish, English
Currency: Surinamese Guilder

Uruguay

Oriental Republic of Uruguay

Uruguay was one of the Argentinean
provinces which sought independence
from Spain. Although it did not support
the idea of joining Argentina, Uruguay
copied its flag emblems. Independence
was recognized on August 25, 1828.
The nine stripes in the Uruguayan
flag—adopted July 11, 1830, and
reminiscent of the Stars and Stripes—
represent the nine departments of the
country. The sun symbolizes the bright
future of the country.

Capital: Montevideo
Area (sq. km): 176,200
Population: 3,400,000
Languages: Spanish
Currency: Uruguayan Peso

Venezuela

Bolivarian Republic of Venezuela

Between 1819 and 1830 Venezuela joined
the federation of Greater Colombia. The
flag's colors—chosen by the liberation
leader Francisco de Miranda—show that
South America (gold) is separated by
an ocean (blue) from hated Spain (red).
Venezuela added seven stars in the
blue stripe, which stand for the
provinces supporting independence.

Capital: Caracas
Area (sq. km): 912,050
Population: 23,600,000
Languages: Spanish
Currency: Bolívar

The people of Chile fly their national flag at a victory rally in Santiago.

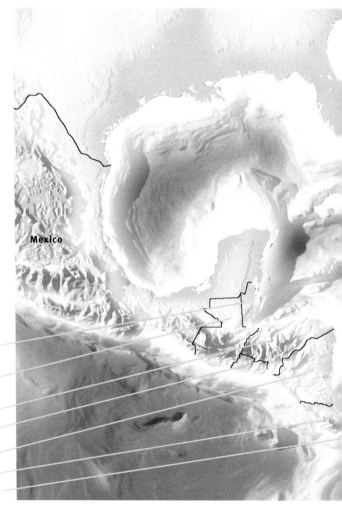

Mexico

Belize

Guatemala

Honduras

El Salvador

Nicaragua

Costa Rica

Panama

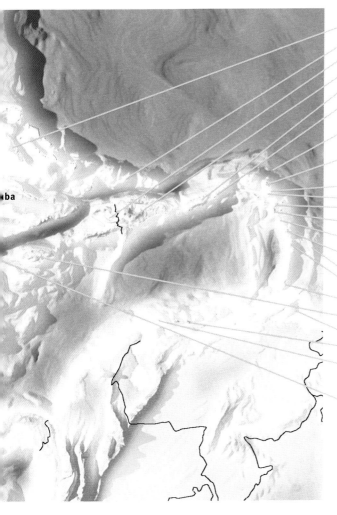

Bahamas

Turks and Caicos Islands

Haiti

Dominican Republic

Puerto Rico
Virgin Islands UK and USA

Anguilla

St. Kitts-Nevis

Antigua and Barbuda

Monserrat
Guadeloupe

Dominica

Martinique

St. Lucia

Barbados

St. Vincent
Grenada

Jamaica

Trinidad and Tobago
Netherlands Antilles

Aruba

Cayman Islands

ba

The flags of the 32 countries in CENTRAL AMERICA can be divided into three categories. In the first category belong the flags of the countries on the ridge between North and South America (which are nearly two centuries old). The second group includes the flags of the Caribbean islands which became independent in the second half of the last century. The third category includes the flags of the British, French, Dutch, and American dependencies in the Caribbean Sea. Out of the 32 political entities in Central America, one third are still administered by a foreign power, which is clearly seen in the design of the flags.

The process of adopting flags started in the first half of the 19th century, when the people of the Central American ridge started to feel unhappy with Spanish rule. The Spaniards colonized this part of the world from the 16th century, showing a great interest in its mineral wealth. Mexico was first to declare its independence in 1821. In its flag choice it honored France, promoter of freedom, equality, and fraternity, although it gave the three vertical bands other colors.

Five areas south of Mexico started to feel unhappy with the Spanish domination and Costa Rica, Nicaragua, Honduras, El Salvador, and Guatemala forged the United Provinces of Central America in 1823. The flag of the United Provinces had three horizontal stripes: blue, white, and blue. The central stripe was charged with the Union's coat of arms. The flag read like a map; the white stripe symbolized the Central American land ridge, the bands at the top and bottom stood for the bordering Pacific and the Atlantic Oceans.

The United Provinces of Central America disintegrated into five independent countries in 1839. All of them acknowledged the union by adopting its flag colors. Only Costa Rica enhanced its blue and white flag with a red stripe; the president, who admired France, wanted a French-looking flag.

The French Tricolore was also used to model the flags of Haiti and the Dominican Republic. Haiti had become a French colony in 1697. After a rebellion in 1803, independence was granted on New Year's Day 1804. By cutting up the French flag and stitching the blue and red bands horizontally, they created their own flag. The neighboring Dominican Republic got its flag on a similar way. Occupied by Haiti, when it became independent in 1844, it cut up a Haitian flag and rearranged the pieces of cloth.

The American Stars and Stripes was used in the design for the flags of Cuba, Puerto Rico, and Panama. Cuba's flag was originally designed in 1848 when the liberation movement wanted to break with Spain and make the island part of the United States. The attempt failed, but for a long time the idea was not given up. The Revolutionary Party of Cuba had a section in Puerto Rico in 1895. They adopted the Cuban flag in reversed colors.

In the 1960s, 1970s, and 1980s many of the Caribbean islands were granted independence. In their search for state symbols, many of these small island states held flag design competitions. The favorite colors were blue, red, yellow, green, and black. The Caribbean Sea is often represented in these flags by the use of blue, which can also refer to the blue skies over the islands. The sandy yellow beaches of islands are illustrated in several flags by the use of yellow stripes and symbols. Green represents the forests and agriculture of the islands. Although there was little blood shed in the road to autonomy, red in most cases refers to the struggle for independence. The ancestors of most of the islanders are of African descent, which is evoked by the use of the black.

The remaining 11 dependencies are governed by a foreign power and nine have their own flag. The French islands Martinique and Guadeloupe have the status of departments and therefore use the Tricolore as the national flag. The five British dependent territories use blue ensigns charged with the local badge. As most of these territories are satisfied with their political status, it is not expected that these flags will change in the near future.

Anguilla

Anguilla is a British Dependent Territory, as indicated by its flag. A blue ensign is charged with the island's arms in the fly and was first hoisted on May 30, 1990. The arms show three orange-colored dolphins, representing unity, strength, and endurance, on a white background. The blue base in the shield symbolizes the Caribbean Sea.

Capital: The Valley
Area (sq. km): 96
Population: 12,600
Languages: English
Currency: East Caribbean Dollar

Antigua and Barbuda

Antiguan artist Reginald Samuel designed the flag of Antigua and Barbuda in 1967, when the country obtained autonomy. It stayed the same at independence from the United Kingdom on November 1, 1981. The sun symbolizes the dawn of a new era; red stands for dynamism, blue for hope, black recalls the African heritage of the people. The "V" is the symbol for victory.

Capital: St. John's
Area (sq. km): 442
Population: 66,500
Languages: English
Currency: East Caribbean Dollar

Aruba

The island of Aruba in the Caribbean Sea was part of The Netherlands Antilles until January 1, 1986, when it obtained "Status Aparte." The adoption of its own flag on March 16, 1976, was the first step toward autonomy. Its UN-blue field represents the sky and sea. The four points of the star indicate the directions the ancestors of the Arubans came from. The yellow stripes symbolize the island's prosperous past and future.

Capital: Oranjestad
Area (sq. km): 193
Population: 95,000
Languages: Dutch, Papiamento
Currency: Aruban Guilder

Bahamas

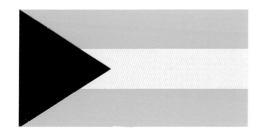

Commonwealth of The Bahamas

The Bahamas became independent on July 10, 1973, and first hoisted its flag. Its design suggests that the islands with their golden beaches, represented by the yellow band, are situated in the Caribbean, which is recalled by the blue stripes. The black triangle represents the strength of the people and their will to develop their country. Black also refers to the African heritage of most of the islanders.

Capital: Nassau
Area (sq. km): 13,950
Population: 311,000
Languages: English
Currency: Bahamian Dollar

Barbados

The design by Grantley Prescod was chosen from 1,029 entries in a Barbados flag design competition, prior to independence on November 30, 1966. The blue panels represent the skies over the island and the surrounding sea. The golden sandy beaches are reflected in the yellow band. The trident, symbol of the mythical sea god Neptune, has a broken shaft to symbolize the break with the colonial past.

Capital: Bridgetown
Area (sq. km): 430
Population: 275,000
Languages: English, Creole
Currency: Barbados Dollar

Belize

The red, white, and blue in the Belizean national flag, introduced at independence from the United Kingdom on September 21, 1981, symbolize the unity of the nation. Evolving from the banner of the leading People's United Party, it includes the white disc with the full coat of arms of Belize, surrounded by a wreath of 50 leaves. This marks the year when the struggle for independence started in 1950.

Capital: Belmopan
Area (sq. km): 23,000
Population: 250,000
Languages: English, Creole, Spanish
Currency: Belizean Dollar

British Virgin Islands

The flag of the British Virgin Islands, which were discovered by Columbus in 1493, was adopted in 1956. The design shows that the archipelago is a British Dependent Territory. It is a blue ensign charged with the territory's arms. The badge shows the island's patron saint, St. Ursula. The 11 lamps surrounding her each represent 1,000 of the 11,000 virgins who, according legend, were martyred along with the patron saint.

Capital: Road Town
Area (sq. km): 150
Population: 6,700
Languages: English
Currency: US Dollar

Cayman Islands

The flag of the Cayman Islands was introduced after the arms were approved on June 2, 1958. The blue ensign design reveals that the islands are a British Dependent Territory. The badge shows three green stars (the islands) in blue and white wavy stripes, representing the Caribbean Sea. The lion above the stars represents England; the turtle on top of the shield shows the significance of these animals to the islands.

Capital: George Town
Area (sq. km): 265
Population: 21,000
Languages: English
Currency: Cayman Islands Dollar

Costa Rica

Republic of Costa Rica

The Central American state of Costa Rica was united with Guatemala, Honduras, El Salvador, and Nicaragua between 1821 and 1839. When this union split, each country adopted a blue and white flag based on the federation flag. The first president of Costa Rica, José Maria Castro, admired the French Revolution and to illustrate this affection added a red stripe to the flag on September 29, 1848.

Capital: San José
Area (sq. km): 51,100
Population: 3,700,000
Languages: Spanish, Creole
Currency: Costa Rican Colòn

Cuba

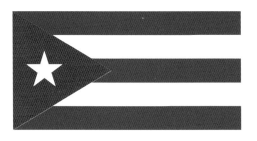

Republic of Cuba

Cuba's flag was designed in 1848, when the then Spanish Caribbean island sought close relations with the United States. The Cuban revolutionary flag was modeled on the American Stars and Stripes. The star represented a new star to be added to "the splendid North American Constellation." It became the national flag on May 20, 1902, when Cuba gained independence. Its nickname is "The Lone Star."

Capital: Havana
Area (sq. km): 110,900
Population: 11,250,000
Languages: Spanish
Currency: Cuban Peso

Dominica

Commonwealth of Dominica

The Sisserou parrot is the national bird of Dominica and features on the center of the flag, which was introduced at independence from the United Kingdom on November 3, 1978. The parrot is encircled with ten green stars, each representing one of the island's parishes. The green field represents the rich verdant forest of the island. The red disc recalls social justice. The yellow, black, and white cross represents belief in God.

Capital: Rousseau
Area (sq. km): 751
Population: 73,000
Languages: English, Creole French
Currency: East Caribbean Dollar

Dominican Republic

Dominican Republic

The Dominican Republic's flag is modeled on that of neighboring Haiti and was made by Juan Pablo Duarte, leader of the Trinitarians who revolted against Haiti. He cut a Haitian flag into four parts, rearranged the pieces, and stitched them on a white cross. The cross symbolizes the Trinitarian independence movement. The flag was introduced at independence on February 27, 1844. The state flag is charged with the coat of arms.

Capital: Santo Domingo
Area (sq. km): 48,500
Population: 8,500,000
Languages: Spanish
Currency: Dominican Republic Peso

El Salvador

Republic of El Salvador

The flag of El Salvador reveals that the country was part of the United Provinces of Central America from 1823 until 1839. Like Guatemala, Honduras, Costa Rica, and Nicaragua, El Salvador's flag is based on the old, common union. Its current design was adopted on May 17, 1912. The white stripe between two blue stripes illustrates how El Salvador is situated in Central America, which is flanked by two oceans.

Capital: San Salvador
Area (sq. km): 21,000
Population: 6,200,000
Languages: Spanish
Currency: Colon

Grenada

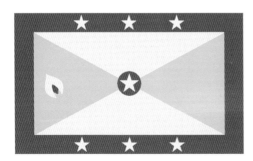

The Caribbean island Grenada is one of the world's biggest nutmeg exporters. When the "Spice Island" gained independence from the United Kingdom on February 7, 1974, it first flew its flag, which expresses the importance of nutmeg to the economy. The central star represents St. George's, the capital. The six stars in the border represent the other parishes. Red stands for vitality, yellow for wisdom, and green for vegetation.

Capital: St. George's
Area (sq. km): 340
Population: 90,000
Languages: English
Currency: East Caribbean Dollar

Guadeloupe

Department of Guadeloupe

Guadeloupe, a group of islands in the West Indies, has been French since 1635 and became an overseas department in 1946. For this reason, its official flag is the French Tricolore. Sometimes a green, white, and red flag charged with a red star is seen in the islands. This is the banner of the independence movement, which is not strongly supported.

Capital: Basse-Terre
Area (sq. km): 1,700
Population: 435,000
Languages: French, Creole
Currency: Euro

Guatemala

Republic of Guatemala

Together with Honduras, Nicaragua, El Salvador, and Costa Rica, Guatemala broke with Spain in 1823. The five countries formed the United Provinces of Central America, which existed until 1839. Guatemala adopted its current flag, modeled on that of the Central American Union, on August 17, 1871. It is the only Central American flag with vertical bands. The blue stripes represents the two oceans, white is for Central America.

Capital: Guatemala
Area (sq. km): 108,900
Population: 12,700,000
Languages: Spanish, Indian
Currency: Quetzal

Haiti

Republic of Haiti

France granted Haiti independence on January 1, 1804. The French Tricolore was torn into three parts to stitch the first Haitian flag. Only the blue and red were stitched together to make a flag in horizontal bands. The white was thrown away. The state flag is charged with the national arms. This flag was abolished during the regime of the Duvalier family (1964–1986).

Capital: Port-au-Prince
Area (sq. km): 27,750
Population: 7,900,000
Languages: French, Creole
Currency: Gourde

Honduras

Republic of Honduras

Honduras joined the United Provinces of Central America in 1823 when it broke with Spanish rule. The Honduras flag was adopted on February 16, 1866, and is modeled on that of the 1823–1839 period. The five stars recall the five states, which formed the United Provinces. Blue is for the oceans around Honduras; white is for Central America.

Capital: Tegucigalpa
Area (sq. km): 112,100
Population: 6,300,000
Languages: Spanish, English
Currency: Lempira

Jamaica

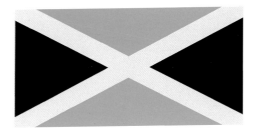

Jamaica's flag was first shown at independence on August 6, 1962. It shows a yellow diagonal cross. Yellow represents the natural wealth and beauty of the sunlight. The black triangles represent hardships, both overcome and yet to be faced. The green triangles symbolize hope and agricultural resources. In short, the flag's optimistic message is: "Hardships there are but the land is green and the sun shineth."

Capital: Kingston
Area (sq. km): 11,000
Population: 2,600,000
Languages: English, Patois
Currency: Jamaican Dollar

Martinique

Department of Martinique

The Caribbean island of Martinique has been French since 1635 and an overseas department since 1946. Its official flag is the French Tricolore. Between 1766 and 1789, Martinique had its own flag, which showed a white cross on a light blue field. In each corner, there was a snake. This historic flag is nowadays often used as a local flag.

Capital: Fort-de-France
Area (sq. km): 1,100
Population: 390,000
Languages: French, Creole
Currency: Euro

Mexico

United Mexican States

Mexico declared its independence from Spain on September 21, 1821. A flag was not adopted until November 2 the same year, when it was decided that the Mexican colors would "forever" be three vertical bands of green, white, and red, with an eagle in the center. The eagle recalls the Aztec legend which said that the people should build their city on the spot where they saw an eagle on a cactus, eating a snake.

Capital: Mexico
Area (sq. km): 1,958,200
Population: 98,500,000
Languages: Spanish, Indian
Currency: Peso

Montserrat

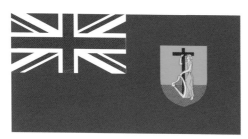

The island Montserrat was settled by Irish immigrants in 1632. The volcanic British Dependent Territory therefore has a flag with Irish connections. The British blue ensign depicts the arms, designed in England in 1909 by Mrs Goodwin. The badge depicts "Lady Erin" playing an Irish harp (Erin is the Irish name for Ireland). Her coat is green, recalling the green of Ireland. The cross symbolizes Christianity.

Capital: Plymouth
Area (sq. km): 100
Population: 5,300
Languages: English
Currency: East Caribbean Dollar

Netherlands Antilles

The flag of the Netherlands Antilles, first adopted on January 1, 1986, reads like a political map. The fact the territory contains five islands with equal rights is recalled by the ring of five stars. The blue stripe in which they feature symbolizes the Caribbean Sea. By the use of the Dutch colors red, white, and blue, the flag reveals that the five islands belong to Holland. The separate islands each have their own flag.

Capital: Willemstad
Area (sq. km): 800
Population: 216,000
Languages: Dutch, English, Papiamento
Currency: Netherlands Antilles Guilder

Nicaragua

Republic of Nicaragua

Nicaragua's flag, adopted on September 4, 1908, is similar to the flags of the neighboring countries Guatemala, Honduras, El Salvador, and Costa Rica, recalling the United Provinces of Central America. The blue stripes represent the Atlantic and Pacific Oceans which border Central America, represented by the white band. Nicaragua's arms are in the white band.

Capital: Managua
Area (sq. km): 130,000
Population: 5,000,000
Languages: Spanish, English
Currency: Córdoba

Panama

Republic of Panama

Panama was originally a Colombian province. With help from the Americans, who were eager to build the Panama Canal, independence was declared on November 3, 1903. On the same day, the new flag, designed by Manuel A. Guerra, (the first President) and based on the Stars and Stripes, was first flown. Quarters and stars are said to represent the rival political factions. White stands for peace.

Capital: Panama City
Area (sq. km): 75,500
Population: 2,900,000
Languages: Spanish, English
Currency: Balboa

Puerto Rico

Commonwealth of Puerto Rico

The flag of Puerto Rico came into official use on July 24, 1952, when the island gained autonomy from the United States. It is modeled on the Cuban flag; the same design, but the colors are reversed. The flag was originally used in 1895 to represent the Puerto Rican section of the Revolutionary Party of Cuba, which sought independence. Both islands worked closely together to overthrow Spanish rule.

Capital: San Juan
Area (sq. km): 8,875
Population: 3,900,000
Languages: Spanish, English
Currency: US Dollar

St. Kitts-Nevis

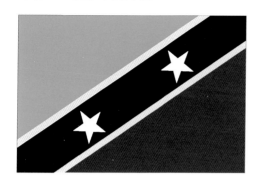

Federation of St. Kitts and Nevis

The islands of St. Kitts and Nevis were granted independence from the United Kingdom on September 19, 1983. The flag, the winning entry to the competition, was designed by Miss Edrice Lewis. Green stands for the fertile islands, yellow for the year round sunshine, black for the African heritage of the people, and red for the struggle from slavery through colonization to independence. The stars represent hope and liberty.

Capital: Basseterre
Area (sq. km): 260
Population: 40,000
Languages: English
Currency: East Caribbean Dollar

St. Lucia

When St. Lucia became independent from the United Kingdom on February 22, 1979, it already flew its own flag. This had been designed in 1967 by the St. Lucian artist Dunstan St. Omer. Blue represents fidelity, the tropical sky, and the surrounding waters. The triangles represent the twin peaks of the volcanic mountains, the Pitons. Yellow stands for prosperity, and black and white for two races living and working in unity.

Capital: Castries
Area (sq. km): 620
Population: 156,000
Languages: English, French Creole
Currency: East Caribbean Dollar

St. Vincent and the Grenadines

St. Vincent is the only Caribbean island state which has replaced its flag since independence on October 27, 1979. It was introduced on October 21, 1985 and has since been called "The Gems." The gems, symbolized by three diamonds in a "V" shape, define St. Vincent and the Grenadines as the gems of the Antilles. The blue panels stand for the Caribbean Sea, yellow is warmth, and green represents the vitality of the people.

Capital: Kingstown
Area (sq. km): 390
Population: 115,000
Languages: English
Currency: East Caribbean Dollar

Trinidad and Tobago

Republic of Trinidad and Tobago

Trinidad and Tobago's national flag was first flown at independence on August 31, 1962. Red represents the vitality of the land and its people, the energy of the sun and the land's wealth. White represents the sea, the purity of aspirations, and the equality of all men. Black stands for the dedication of the people joined together by one strong bond. Red, white, and black represent the elements of earth, water, and fire.

Capital: Port-of-Spain
Area (sq. km): 5,100
Population: 1,300,000
Languages: English
Currency: Trinidad and Tobago Dollar

Turks and Caicos Islands

The British Dependent Territory Turks and Caicos Islands have a traditional blue ensign depicted with the arms of the archipelago in the fly. Queen Elizabeth II approved the flag design on November 7, 1968. The badge displays the local Turk's head cactus and a crawfish and a seashell. These refer to the fishing industry, which forms the main export products of the islands.

Capital: Cockburn Town
Area (sq. km): 430
Population: 23,500
Languages: English
Currency: US Dollar

US Virgin Islands

Virgin Islands of the United States

The flag of the United States Virgin Islands, designed by Rear-Admiral Sumner E.W. Kittelle, US Navy, was adopted on May 17, 1921. Upon a white field it shows the American eagle in yellow with the shield of the United States on its breast. In one claw it holds three arrows, representing the main islands. In the other claw is a twig of laurel. The letters "VI" supporting the eagle stand for Virgin Islands.

Capital: Charlotte Amalie
Area (sq. km): 350
Population: 116,000
Languages: English
Currency: US Dollar

Alaska

Yukon

Nor
Ter

Nisga'a

British
Coumbia

Albe

Washington

Oregon

Idaho

Montana

Wyoming

N. Dakota

S. Dakota

Minnesota

Wisconsin

Michigan

Maine

Vermont

N.H

New York

Mass
Con

R.I.

Nevada

Utah

California

Arizona

Colorado

New Mexico

Nebraska

Kansas

Iowa

Illinois

Missouri

Oklahoma

Arkansas

Texas

Indiana

Ohio

Kentucky

Tennessee

Mississippi

Louisiana

Alabama

Pennsylvania

N.J.

Maryland

Delaware

W. Virginia

Virginia

N. Carolina

S. Carolina

Georgia

Florida

N.H=New Hampshire
Mass=Massachusetts
Con = Connecticut

N.J. =New Jersey
R.I. =Rhode Island

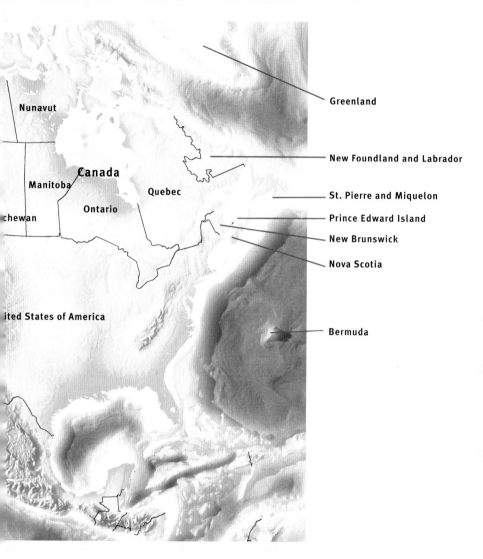

Nunavut

Canada

Manitoba

Quebec

Ontario

chewan

ited States of America

Greenland

New Foundland and Labrador

St. Pierre and Miquelon

Prince Edward Island

New Brunswick

Nova Scotia

Bermuda

The United States and Canada cover most of the vast territory of NORTH AMERICA. They are surrounded by a few islands, which are administered by European states. These are the last remains of what began in about 1500, when the European countries showed an interest in this "New World."

North America saw thousands of immigrants arriving from the Old World, who brought their old world symbols with them, and thereby introduced flags to the continent. When the sons and daughters of the first immigrants needed their own symbols, they looked to the old European flags for ideas. During the revolution against the British in 1776, the Americans modeled their sign of liberty on the striped flag of the British East India Company. The result, the Stars and Stripes, has since become the world's best-known flag. It strikingly represents freedom and liberty while reminding us that out of 13 colonies, 50 states have grown and united.

In 1780, the Union authorized each state to use a state flag. Early versions were in fact military banners of the regiments of each state. Beginning in the original 13 states, this tradition was copied by new states when they entered the Union. These early flags showed a similar pattern. They were buff, later blue, with the coat of arms or seal in the center and were mainly used in the army and on the battlefields. They were not flown from the legislative buildings as is the case nowadays.

Texas and California were the first states to introduce state flags as we know them today. At the beginning of the 19th century, both states were Mexican, but most Texans and Californians were not happy with this situation. They seceded, adopting their own flags as a sign of independence.

The flag of the United States, seen here hanging in Grant's Tomb, New York, is the most recognized

flag in the world.

The Texan flag was modeled on the Stars and Stripes. Texas and California later joined the Union and kept their independent flags for use as state flags.

The American Civil War (1861–1865) gave most of the Southern States the flags they still use today, or variants of them. Most were first used as flags of independence, before joining the Confederation. Some of these flags have recently come under fire, as many African-Americans regard them as symbols of slavery. Georgia revised its state flag in 2001 to include references to all its historical flags.

During World War I, the "Daughters of the American Revolution" promoted the notion of a state flag to those states that did not have one. The patriotic women's organization encouraged the sending of copies of state flags to soldiers fighting in the French trenches. The need for individual state flags became apparent. Most of the flags designed at this time were modeled on the flags of the other states, which had their seal or coat of arms on a blue field. For this reason 26 of the 50 state flags look very similar, so most of the flags have the name of the state imprinted on them in bold letters. Some states are currently considering changing their flag to a more distinguishable design.

Canada adopted its current flag in 1965, in an attempt to keep the country together. The French-speaking majority of Quebec did not feel at home in the mainly English speaking Canada. The Dominion, which had come into existence in 1867, used a red ensign as the national flag, charged by a miniature version of the British Union Flag. Quebec was the first province to use its own flag, in 1948, to distinguish itself from the rest of Canada.

For some provinces, such as British Columbia and Nova Scotia, Quebec's move was the sign to make use of old royal rights to use the provincial arms on their flags. Not happy with the change of the national flags in 1965, Manitoba and Ontario immediately adopted provincial flags, which looked like the abolished Canadian flag.

The centennial celebrations in 1967 were the signal for the remaining provinces and territories to design their own flags. When Nunavut was established on April 1, 1999, as Canada's youngest entity, the first act adopted by the territorial assembly was the design of the flag. The Indian Nisga'a Nation was granted autonomy within the province of British Columbia in May 2000. Its flag design was given the highest priority and its adoption might be the start of creating other First Nation flags.

Bermuda

Bermuda, a cluster of some 100 islands, is one of the few remaining dependencies of the United Kingdom. Unlike other British possessions, which fly blue ensigns, Bermuda has a red version. This symbolizes that the island was colonized by the Bermuda Company after Sir George Somers was shipwrecked there on his way to Virginia. This historical scene is depicted in the arms in the flag's fly.

Capital: Hamilton
Area (sq. km): 53
Population: 65,000
Languages: English
Currency: Bermuda Dollar

Greenland

Greenland's flag, designed by the artist Thue Christiansen, was first hoisted on March 21, 1985. The world's largest island is a Danish territory. The white part at the top symbolizes the inland ice. The red semicircle represents the deep fjords and the sun. The surrounding sea is expressed with the flag's red lower part. The white semicircle stands for the ice sheets in the sea.

Capital: Nuuk (Godthåb)
Area (sq. km): 2,175,600
Population: 57,000
Languages: Danish, Inuit
Currency: Danish Kroner

St. Pierre and Miquelon

Territorial Collectivity of St. Pierre and Miquelon

The small islands of St. Pierre and Miquelon are French possessions off the coast of Newfoundland. In 1985, they became a territorial collectivity, a political status somewhere between that of a department and a territory. For this reason, the legal flag of the islands is the French Tricolore. Sometimes a local flag is seen, which is a heraldic banner of the local arms.

Capital: St. Pierre
Area (sq. km): 240
Population: 6,500
Languages: French
Currency: Euro

Canada

The maple leaf in Canada's flag is an old Canadian emblem. It was honored with a central position on the flag when Canada adopted its current flag on February 15, 1965. Canada became a nation July 1, 1867, and first flew a British-styled red ensign. This color was copied in Canada's current flag. The two red bars symbolize the Atlantic and the Pacific. The white (snow) panel with the maple leaf represents Canada.

Capital: Ottawa
Area (sq. km): 9,922,330
Population: 31,500,000
Languages: English, French, indigenous languages
Currency: Canadian Dollar

Alberta

The province of Alberta was created out of the Northwest Territories on September 1, 1905. King Edward VII granted the province its arms on May 30, 1907. It shows the cross of St. George and a typical Alberta landscape. Alberta felt the need of a flag in 1967 at the commemoration of the Centennial of the Confederation. It was made official on June 1, 1968. The blue is royal ultramarine blue.

Capital: Edmonton
Area (sq. km): 661,185
Population: 3,065,000

British Columbia

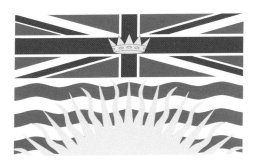

The provincial flag of British Columbia was adopted March 20, 1960. It is the banner of the provincial arms, granted on March 31, 1906. The upper part is the British Union Flag, symbolizing the colonial origins. The setting sun and the blue and white wavy stripes represent the geographical location between the Rocky Mountains and the Pacific.

Capital: Victoria
Area (sq. km): 948,596
Population: 4,100,000

Manitoba

The flag of the province of Manitoba was proclaimed on May 12, 1966, the date in 1870 when the Manitoba Act was given royal assent. Manitoba adopted this British-styled flag, just as Canada had abandoned the same style. Manitoba opposed this and felt it should honor its British past. Manitoba's coat of arms, granted on May 10, 1905, by King Edward VII, shows a buffalo standing on a rock.

Capital: Winnipeg
Area (sq. km): 650,087
Population: 1,155,000

New Brunswick

The flag of New Brunswick is made of the arms assigned to the province on May 26, 1868. It was, however, proclaimed on February 24, 1965, just after Canada got its current flag. The yellow lion in the top of the flag is an English lion and symbolizes New Brunswick's ties with England. The galley ship recalls shipbuilding, which was once an important industry. Seafaring was also important to New Brunswick.

Capital: Fredericton
Area (sq. km): 73,436
Population: 760,000

Newfoundland and Labrador

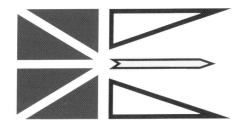

Newfoundland and Labrador, Britain's oldest colony, became the tenth Canadian province on March 31, 1949, and it flew the British Union Flag. The colors in the current flag, which were adopted on May 28, 1980, try to reveal everything about the province. White symbolizes snow and ice; blue the sea; red human effort; and yellow confidence in the future. The two red triangles represent the mainland and islands of the province.

Capital: St. John's
Area (sq. km): 404,517
Population: 535,000

Nisga'a

Nisga'a Nation

The Indian Nisga'a Nation has had autonomy within British Colombia since May 2000. The flag, the result of a public competition won by Lloyd McDames and Peter McKay, was adopted on April 24, 2001. Red, white, and black are the traditional Nisga'a colors. The circle in the white stripe represents a rainbow. The hayatskw, a copper shield, symbolizes the history of the Nisga'a Nation.

Capital: New Aiyansh
Area (sq. km): 2,000
Population: 5,500

Northwest Territories

The flag of the Northwest Territories was modeled on the Canadian flag. It was adopted on January 1, 1969. The flag includes the territorial shield, the upper third of which represents the polar ice pack with a wavy blue line representing the Northwest Passage. The lower part represents flora and fauna. The flag's blue panels stand for the lakes and waters of the territory. The central panel represents the snow and ice of the North.

Capital: Yellowknife
Area (sq. km): 1,171,918
Population: 41,000

Nova Scotia

Nova Scotia has the oldest Canadian provincial flag. It was derived from the arms granted by King Charles I in 1625. By Royal Charter, King George V granted Nova Scotia the right to use the arms copied on a banner on January 19, 1929. Nova Scotia means "new Scotland," which is why it uses St. Andrew's cross in reversed colors. In the center is the shield of the royal arms of Scotland.

Capital: Halifax
Area (sq. km): 55,491
Population: 945,000

Nunavut

Nunavut was created on April 1, 1999, from a vast part of the Northwest Territories. The flag first unveiled that day was created from ideas submitted from all parts of the territory: blue and yellow symbolize the riches of the sea, sky, and land and red refers to Canada. The inuksuk in the center is a stone monument, which guides the people on the land and marks sacred places. The star is the leading North Star.

Capital: Iqaluit
Area (sq. km): 1,994,000
Population: 29,000

Ontario

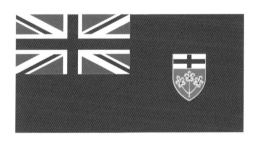

Ontario did not like Canada's flag change from a British red ensign design to its current design in 1965. Therefore, it adopted a provincial flag based on the abolished Canadian flag as a sign of protest. In the fly is the provincial shield, which shows the English St. George cross and a green shield with three yellow Canadian maple leaves. The flag was adopted on April 14, 1965.

Capital: Toronto
Area (sq. km): 1,068,582
Population: 11,900,000

Prince Edward Island

The provincial flag of Prince Edward Island, adopted by the Act of Legislature on 24 March, 1964, is modeled after the coat of arms. On the three free sides it is bordered by alternate bands of white and red. The top of the flag shows the English lion to represent the English heritage. The lower part shows an island with a mature oak tree, recalling England, and three saplings, representing Prince Edward Island.

Capital: Charlottetown
Area (sq. km): 5,657
Population: 140,000

Quebec

In 1948 French-speaking Quebec was not happy with the British-styled Canadian national flag. By Order of the Lieutenant Governor in Council on January 21, 1948, the province adopted its own distinct flag, the fleur-de-lis, which recalls Quebec's entirely French heritage. The white cross on the blue field was taken from an ancient French military banner, and the fleurs-de-lis are symbolic of the old pre-revolutionary France.

Capital: Quebec City
Area (sq. km): 1,540,680
Population: 7,420,000

Saskatchewan

Saskatchewan became a province on September 1, 1905, and its flag was adopted on March 31, 1969. The upper green stripe symbolizes the forested areas in the north. The grain areas are represented in the lower yellow stripe. In the fly is the provincial floral emblem, the western red lily. The provincial shield is depicted in the upper quarter. It shows the English lion and the wheat sheaves, representing agriculture.

Capital: Regina
Area (sq. km): 652,900
Population: 1,025,000

Yukon Territory

The Yukon Territory was created in June 1898 from the Northwest Territories. Its flag was designed by Lynn Lambert and adopted by the Territorial Council on December 1, 1967. The green band represents the green taiga forests, the winter snow is recalled by the white band, and the northern waters by the deep blue band. The provincial arms are decorated with the provincial flower, the purple fireweed.

Capital: Whitehorse
Area (sq. km): 482,515
Population: 30,000

United States of America

The Stars and Stripes of the USA is the world's best-known flag. It shows that in 1776, the country had 13 states by the red and white stripes. Since 1959, the USA has had 50 states, which is expressed by the 50 white stars in the blue canton. This leaves space for future stars when other states decide to join the USA. The colors red, white, and blue were originally taken from the British Union Flag.

Capital: Washington DC
Area (sq. km): 9,157,000
Population: 278,000,000
Languages: English, Spanish
Currency: US Dollar

Alabama

The Yellowhammer State

The Alabama flag is modeled on the Battle Flag of the Confederacy. It shows a red diagonal cross on a white field and was created on February 16, 1895. Legislation failed to rule on the dimensions of the state flag. For this reason, there have been several versions of the flag in use. When Alabama seceded the Union on January 11, 1861, it adopted a blue flag with a picture of Liberty holding a flag and a sword.

Capital: Montgomery
Area (sq. km): 131,443
Population: 4,500,000

Alaska

The Last Frontier

When 13-year-old orphan Benny Benson designed the Alaskan flag in 1927, it was still a territory. Benny received a reward of $1,000. His explanation for the design was: "The blue is for the Alaskan sky and the forget-me-not, an Alaskan flower. The North Star is for the future state of the Union. The Dipper is for the Great Bear—symbolizing strength." Alaska became the 49th state of the Union on January 3, 1959.

Capital: Juneau
Area (sq. km): 1,477,268
Population: 621,000

Arizona

The Grand Canyon State

The Arizona flag was first flown at a national rifle shooting match in Ohio in 1911, when Arizona was a territory. Colonel Adjutant General Charles W. Harris designed it. Red and yellow represent the Spanish past and the setting sun over the desert. The blue half represents the Union. The copper colored star recalls the mineral wealth. Arizona became the 48th state in 1912 and the flag became official on February 27, 1917.

Capital: Phoenix
Area (sq. km): 294,333
Population: 4,900,000

Arkansas

The Natural State

Arkansas felt the need for a flag in 1912 when a new battleship, the USS *Arkansas*, was commissioned. It was adopted on February 26, 1913, and designed by Miss Willie K. Hocker. She modeled it on the Battle Flag of the Confederacy. The 25 white stars indicate that Arkansas was the 25th state of the Union. The diamond signifies Arkansas is the only diamond-producing state of the Union.

Capital: Little Rock
Area (sq. km): 134,875
Population: 2,600,000

California

The Golden State

Americans who wanted to break away from Mexico and set up an independent republic of California first hoisted the flag on June 14, 1846, at Sonoma. It was declared the official flag of the State of California on February 3, 1911. White symbolizes purity, the red in the stripe and star are for courage. The star also represents sovereignty and the grizzly bear great strength.

Capital: Sacramento
Area (sq. km): 403,971
Population: 33,500,000

Colorado

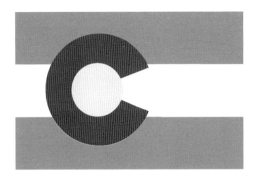

Centennial State

Andrew C. Carson designed the Colorado state flag, which was adopted on June 5, 1911. Colorado, which is Spanish for the color red, was admitted to the Union on August 1, 1876. The capital "C" is for Colorado; its red color recalls the Colorado soil. The yellow disc represents the gold to be found in the mountains. White and blue represent the Union; blue also stands for the blue skies and white for the mountain snows.

Capital: Denver
Area (sq. km): 268,658
Population: 4,100,000

Connecticut

The Constitution State

In the 19th century, a flag of blue with the state arms came into use. Following pressure by the "Daughters of the American Revolution," it became the official state flag on May 29, 1895. The vines on the state arms recall the colonists who transformed a wilderness into cultivation. The Latin motto "Qui Transtulit Sustinet" also refers to the colonists: "He Who Transplanted Still Sustains."

Capital: Hartford
Area (sq. km): 12,550
Population: 3,400,000

Delaware

DECEMBER 7, 1787

The First State

Delaware has a flag of colonial blue with a diamond of buff color in which the state arms are placed. The date, December 7, 1787, indicates the day when Delaware ratified the federal constitution as the first state of the Union. Colonial blue and buff were the colors of the Continental uniform in the Revolutionary War and refer to the uniform of George Washington. The Delaware state flag was adopted on July 24, 1913.

Capital: Dover
Area (sq. km): 5,063
Population: 765,000

Florida

The Sunshine State

Florida has had six flags since the first was raised on June 25, 1845, a couple of months after its admission to the Union as the 27th state. After the Civil War, Florida adopted a plain white flag with the Great Seal of the state on it. As this flag lacked any color, in 1899, Governor Francis Fleming promoted the addition of a red diagonal cross, recalling the Spanish era and the Confederate States.

Capital: Tallahassee
Area (sq. km): 139,853
Population: 15,500,000

Georgia

The Peach State

The state flag adopted by Georgia on January 31, 2001, is a compromise. It's an amalgamation of stars, words, numbers, banners, and five historical flags that flew over the state. It was designed by 82-year-old architect Cecil Alexander and replaced the Georgia flag modeled on the Battle Flag of the Confederacy that had been seen as symbol of slavery. In the flag's center is the great seal of Georgia.

Capital: Atlanta
Area (sq. km): 150,010
Population: 7,900,000

Hawaii

The Aloha State

Hawaii adopted its current flag on May 25, 1845, when it became independent. It was modeled on an earlier design and presented to the Legislative Assembly by Captain Hunt of the Baselisk. The Union Flag represented the friendly relationship between the United Kingdom and the Kingdom of Hawaii. The eight stripes represent the eight main islands. Hawaii became the 50th state of the Union on August 21, 1959.

Capital: Honolulu
Area (sq. km): 16,637
Population: 1,200,000

Idaho

The Gem State

Idaho was admitted to the Union in 1890. Its first flag was adopted in 1907 and was changed twice before settling on its current design on March 1, 1957. On a blue field is the great seal of Idaho, the only American great seal designed by a woman, Emma Edwards Green. The seal shows a scenic landscape, including the River Shoshone. The scroll underneath the seal tells that it is the flag of the "State of Idaho."

Capital: Boise
Area (sq. km): 214,325
Population: 1,300,000

Illinois

The Prairie State

The state flag of Illinois became official on July 6, 1915. It is a simple representation of the great seal of Illinois on a white flag. It was designed by Miss Lucy Derwant of the Rockford chapter of the "Daughters of the American Revolution." Its identity was often questioned, so on July 1, 1970, the word Illinois was added. The eagle flag has a scroll in its beak declaring: "State Sovereignty—National Union."

Capital: Springfield
Area (sq. km): 143,987
Population: 12,200,000

Indiana

The Hoosier State

Paul Hadley submitted the prize-winning design of the Indiana state flag competition in 1916, sponsored by the Indiana "Daughters of the American Revolution." The torch represents liberty and enlightenment. The 13 stars in the outer circle represent the original 13 states of the Union. Indiana was the 19th state admitted to the Union, which is represented by the six stars in the inner circle.

Capital: Indianapolis
Area (sq. km): 92,904
Population: 6,000,000

Iowa

The Hawkeye State

Iowa's origin as part of the Louisiana Purchase from France is reflected in the state flag, which is modeled on the French Tricolore. The blue, white, and red flag was adopted on March 29, 1921. In the center panel is an eagle from the state seal. In its beaks it holds a scroll which says: "Our Liberties We Prize and Our Rights We Will Maintain." Below the eagle, "Iowa" is written in capital letters.

Capital: Des Moines
Area (sq. km): 144,716
Population: 2,900,000

Kansas

The Sunflower State

The Kansas state flag was adopted on March 23, 1927, but, as it looked like many other American state flags, the word "Kansas" was added on June 30, 1963. In the middle of the blue flag is the Kansas Great Seal, which shows a historical landscape near the Kansas River. It also shows a constellation of 34 stars to recall that Kansas was the 34th state of the Union. The motto "Ad Astra per Aspera" means "To the Stars through Difficulties."

Capital: Topeka
Area (sq. km): 211,922
Population: 2,750,000

Kentucky

The Bluegrass State

After ten years of indecision over the design, the Kentucky flag was approved on March 26, 1928. In the center of a navy blue field is a white disc with "two friends embracing," representing the US and Kentucky. The friend's pledge: "United we Stand, Divided we Fall." As the flag looked like many American flags, the state name was added in an arc above the disc on June 14, 1962, together with some goldenrod, the state flower.

Capital: Frankfort
Area (sq. km): 102,907
Population: 4,000,000

Louisiana

The Pelican State

Louisiana was purchased on April 30, 1803, in one of the greatest real estate deals in history. The United States paid France $15 million for the Louisiana purchase. The Louisiana State Legislature approved the state flag on July 1, 1912. It depicts the state bird, the Easter Brown Pelican, in white on a blue field, feeding its young. It also shows the state motto "Union, Justice & Confidence."

Capital: Baton Rouge
Area (sq. km): 112,836
Population: 4,400,000

Maine

The Pine Tree State

Maine became a state on March 15, 1820. Its flag dates from March 23, 1909, when the full arms were placed on a blue field. The main feature on the shield is a pine tree, commemorating the white pines used in ancient shipbuilding. Above the shield is the North Star with the motto "Dirigo" (I direct), recalling that Maine was for a long time the most northerly state. The shield supporters are a sailor and a farmer.

Capital: Augusta
Area (sq. km): 79,939
Population: 1,300,000

Maryland

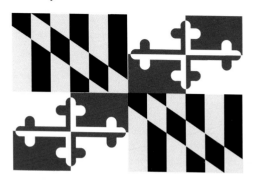

The Old Line State

Maryland's standard was adopted on March 9, 1904. Without doubt, it is the most distinctive state flag of the Union. It is taken from the seal of Sir George Calvert, the first Lord Baltimore, who was chartered to colonize Maryland. The yellow and black quarters are taken from the arms of the Calvert family. The quarters with red and white Greek crosses recall the arms of Calvert's mother's family, the Crosslands.

Capital: Annapolis
Area (sq. km): 25,316
Population: 5,200,000

Massachusetts

The Bay State

The state flag of Massachusetts is among the oldest in the United States. It is based on a militia flag of 1787. It became the official state flag on March 18, 1908. The Indian man on the shield recalls the people living in Massachusetts before the English colonists came. The star signifies Massachusetts is an American state. The Latin inscription means "By the Sword We Seek Peace, but Peace only under Liberty."

Capital: Boston
Area (sq. km): 20,300
Population: 6,200,000

Michigan

The Wolverine State

Michigan's first flag was displayed in 1837 and showed the seal. On August 1, 1911, it was decided that "The state flag shall be blue charged with the arms of the State." These are modeled on the arms of the Hudson Bay Company. The shield is supported by a moose and an elk and depicts a man at the bank of one of five Michigan lakes before a rising sun. The two Latin mottos mean "From many, one" and "I will defend."

Capital: Lansing
Area (sq. km): 147,136
Population: 9,900,000

Minnesota

The North Star State

Minnesota is one of the 26 states with a blue flag charged with the arms or seal. There is a strong movement to revise the flag into a simple, powerful design. The current flag was approved March 19, 1957. It shows the state's seal placed on a white disc and is surrounded by 19 stars, which is a reminder that Minnesota was the 19th state of the Union (after the original 13) when the seal was designed in 1858.

Capital: St. Paul
Area (sq. km): 206,207
Population: 4,800,000

Mississippi

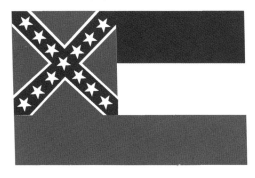

The Magnolia State

The Mississippi flag, which was approved on February 7, 1894, and designed by General W.T. Martin, is divided into three horizontal stripes, blue, white, and red. These represent the national American colors. In the canton is the Confederate Battle flag with 13 white stars. A proposal to alter the state flag on April 17, 2001, as it bears a symbol of slavery, was turned down by 65 percent of the voters.

Capital: Jackson
Area (sq. km): 121,506
Population: 2,800,000

Missouri

Show Me State

Mrs. Marie Elizabeth Oliver, wife of the former state Governor R.B. Watkins, designed Missouri's flag which was adopted on March 22, 1913. It consists of three horizontal stripes of red, white, and blue. These colors represented valor, purity, and justice. In the center of the flag is the state coat of arms, circled by a blue band with 24 stars, indicating Missouri was the 24th state of the Union in 1821.

Capital: Jefferson City
Area (sq. km): 178,446
Population: 5,500,000

Montana

The Treasure State

The original state flag of Montana was made in 1898 for the first territorial Montana infantry. These volunteers wanted a symbol to carry with them in the Spanish-American War. On a blue field the flag, which became the official state flag on February 27, 1905, displays the great seal of Montana. The landscape bears a scroll with the word "Oro y Plata" (Gold and Silver). On July 1, 1981, the state name was added to the flag.

Capital: Helena
Area (sq. km): 376,991
Population: 850,000

Nebraska

The Cornhusker State

Although established on April 2, 1925, Nebraska's state flag was officially adopted in 1963. It was described as: "A reproduction of the great seal of the state charged on the center in gold and silver on a field of national blue." The great seal pictures a landscape in which a smith works with hammer and anvil. The scroll reads: "Equality before the law." There has been a hymn to the flag—"Flag Song of Nebraska"—since 1963.

Capital: Lincoln
Area (sq. km): 199,113
Population: 1,700,000

Nevada

The Silver State

Nevada has had three flags in its history. The current flag was adopted on March 26, 1929. Official specifications were laid down by law on June 8, 1991. Its main color is blue, with a wreath in the canton. Between the points of the star the state name is spelled out. A scroll with the motto "Battle Born" is above the star, recalling that Nevada entered the Union during the Civil War. The wreath is made of sagebrush, the state flower.

Capital: Carson City
Area (sq. km): 284,396
Population: 1,850,000

New Hampshire

The Granite State

New Hampshire is one of the 26 states with a blue flag charged with the great seal of the state. It shows the sailing ship *Raleigh* on the stocks. It was one of the first vessels of the US Navy, launched in 1776. The flag was used from 1792 as a military banner. It was adopted as state flag on January 1, 1932, when a laurel interspersed with nine stars was added to recall New Hampshire was the ninth state to enter the Union.

Capital: Concord
Area (sq. km): 23,231
Population: 1,250,000

New Jersey

The Garden State

General George Washington indirectly ordered the flag of New Jersey. He declared in 1779 that the flag of the state troops should be of buff and Jersey blue. He recalled in this order the Dutch who originally settled New Jersey as both colors figured in the Dutch insignia. New Jersey approved this flag on March 28, 1896, as the state flag. Liberty and Ceres (the goddess of agriculture) support New Jersey's arms on the flag.

Capital: Trenton
Area (sq. km): 19,215
Population: 8,200,000

New Mexico

The Land of Enchantment

The state flag of New Mexico is a combination of the ancient sun symbol of the Zia Indians and the Spanish colors red and yellow. For the Zia Indians the sun is a sacred symbol. They have recently asked for compensation for the use of the symbol. The flag was adopted on March 15, 1925, after a state-wide competition. Dr. Harry Mera submitted the winning design. He copied the sun from an ancient vase.

Capital: Santa Fé
Area (sq. km): 314,334
Population: 1,800,000

New York

The Empire State

New York's flag is blue charged with the coat of arms. It became official on April 2, 1901, with the abolition of the old militia buff flag. The arms rest in the center of the flag with the motto "Excelsior" (Ever Upward). The shield shows a landscape with a rising sun. Two women, representing Liberty and Justice, support the arms. Liberty holds a liberty cap while the blindfolded Justice holds a sword and scales.

Capital: Albany
Area (sq. km): 122,310
Population: 18,500,000

North Carolina

The Old North State

When North Carolina seceded the Union in 1861 it adopted a blue flag with a "V" and a star. After the state was back in the Union, it was made part of the current state flag, which was adopted on March 9, 1885. The dates on the banners recall the "Mecklenburg Declaration of Independence."

Capital: Raleigh
Area (sq. km): 126,180
Population: 7,750,000

North Dakota

The Peace Garden State

North Dakota's state flag bears a modified version of the American coat of arms. It is based on a banner carried by the First North Dakota Volunteers in the Spanish-American War in 1895. The military banner was adopted as state flag on March 3, 1911. The only change made at that time was the change of the wording of the banner below the eagle. "North Dakota" replaced "First North Dakota Infantry."

Capital: Bismarck
Area (sq. km): 178,695
Population: 650,000

Ohio

The Buckeye State

The swallowtail shape of Ohio's state flag is unique among the flags of the American states. It was designed by John Eisenmann and adopted on May 9, 1902. The shape of the flag and blue triangle represents the hills and valleys of Ohio. The red and white stripes are the state's roads and waterways. The 17 stars recall that Ohio was the 17th state of the Union. The white circle with a red center suggests an "O" for Ohio.

Capital: Columbus
Area (sq. km): 106,067
Population: 11,500,000

Oklahoma

The Sooner State

The blue field of the Oklahoma flag signifies devotion. The buffalo rawhide shield is symbolic of defensive strength, yielding always to the olive branch and the peace pipe, which represent the love and peace of a united people. The six crosses on the shield are Indian symbols of stars. The shield is fringed with seven eagle feathers. The flag, designed by Louise F. Fluk, was adopted May 9, 1941.

Capital: Oklahoma City
Area (sq. km): 177,877
Population: 3,500,000

Oregon

The Beaver State

The Oregon state flag is navy blue and has yellow illustrations and lettering. The bold letters "State of Oregon" are added for identity. In the center of the flag is the shield from the state's great seal, supported by 33 stars. These recall Oregon became the 33th state of the Union in 1859. The reverse side of the flag depicts a beaver, reminding Oregon's nickname is the Beaver State.

Capital: Salem
Area (sq. km): 248,646
Population: 3,400,000

Pennsylvania

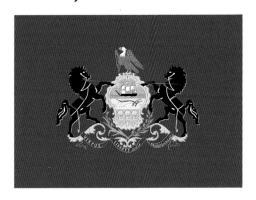

The Keystone State

On June 13, 1907, the Pennsylvania General Assembly decided its flag should be the same color as the blue in the flag of the United States, charged with the full coat of arms of the Commonwealth. The arms were designed by Caleb Lownes of Philadephia in 1778. In a nutshell it tells Pennsylvania's history—how settlers came by ship, and how they worked in the fields that resulted in successful harvests.

Capital: Harrisburg
Area (sq. km): 116,083
Population: 12,200,000

Rhode Island

The Ocean State

The regiments of Rhode Island carried the colors white and blue during the American Revolution, the War of 1812, and the Mexican War. These regimental colors were recalled when the state flag was adopted on May 19, 1897. The anchor is a symbol of hope. The 13 stars represent the original American states, of which Rhode Island was the smallest.

Capital: Providence
Area (sq. km): 2,707
Population: 1,000,000

South Carolina

The Palmetto State

A blue banner with a white crescent was introduced in 1775 by Colonel William Moultree to represent South Carolina's regiments. When South Carolina seceded the Union in 1860, it needed a flag. It readopted the old regimental colors, adding a palmetto on January 28, 1861, as a national flag. The palmetto was to recall Moultree's heroic defense of the palmetto-log on Sullivan's Islands against the British in June 1776.

Capital: Columbia
Area (sq. km): 77,988
Population: 3,900,000

South Dakota

The Mount Rushmore State

South Dakota's flag is blue with the great seal of the state in the center. It became official on March 11, 1963, when it superseded a flag that had been official since July 1, 1909. However, this flag had two different sides and was too costly to produce. The seal is an allegorical landscape showing industry and agriculture and the motto "Under God the People Rule." Around the seal the name and nickname of the state is written.

Capital: Pierre
Area (sq. km): 196,571
Population: 750,000

Tennessee

The Volunteer State

Tennessee's state flag was designed by LeRoy Reeves of the Third Regiment, Tennessee Infantry. He was inspired by the flag of the Confederacy. It was adopted officially on April 17, 1905. The three stars represent the three divisions of the state. They are bound together by the endless circle of the blue field. The blue bar is purely decorative, the white bar is to contrast the crimson and blue.

Capital: Nashville
Area (sq. km): 106,759
Population: 5,600,000

Texas

The Lone Star State

Between 1836 and December 29, 1845, when it joined the Union, Texas was an independent country. Its current Lone Star Flag was approved on January 25, 1839, and was inspired by the flag of the United States. The star signifies that Texas felt alone in the Mexican Confederation and that the star of liberty was rising. The red bar signifies bravery, blue indicates loyalty, and white means purity.

Capital: Austin
Area (sq. km): 678,358
Population: 20,500,000

Utah

The Beehive State

The beehive was the emblem of the Mormons, the original settlers of Utah. The flag was adopted on March 11, 1913. In the center is the great seal, which depicts a beehive, flowers, American flags, and an eagle. The dates 1847 and 1896 are important in Utah's history. In 1847, the Mormons migrated to the territory and in 1896 Utah gained statehood. On three sides, the flag is surrounded by golden fringes.

Capital: Salt Lake City
Area (sq. km): 212,816
Population: 2,200,000

Vermont

The Green Mountain State

For a long time Vermont used the American flag with the addition of its name as its state flag. However, Vermont regiments in the Civil War, the Spanish-American War, and World War I carried blue banners with the coat of arms of the state and the Governor also used such a flag. By the law of March 26, 1923, this flag became the official flag of Vermont. The scene on the coat of arms recalls local agriculture, dairy, lumber industries, and the marble quarries.

Capital: Montpelier
Area (sq. km): 23,956
Population: 600,000

Virginia

The Old Dominion State

Immediately after the act of secession from the Union on April 30, 1861, Virginia adopted its flag. It is blue with Virginia's seal in the center on a white disc. The seal records, in a classical style, how good triumphs over evil. Pictured on the seal is Virtue (Virginia's emblem), the victor over Tyranny, represented by the man lying on the ground. The motto "Sic Semper Tyrannis" means "Thus Always to Tyrants."

Capital: Richmond
Area (sq. km): 102,558
Population: 6,900,000

Washington

The Evergreen State

After they had discovered the state of Washington did not have a flag, the "Daughters of the American Revolution" designed one in 1915. They fabricated a green flag with the colored seal of the state in the center. Green represented the Evergreen State, the seal showed George Washington, after whom the state is named. It took until June 7, 1923, until the flag was officially adopted by the state legislature.

Capital: Olympia
Area (sq. km): 172,445
Population: 5,800,000

West Virginia

The Mountain State

The coat of arms of West Virginia is prominently displayed on a pure white flag, which is bordered on four sides by a blue strip. The state flower, rhododendron or Big Laurel, wreathes the shield. The coat of arms shows a miner and a farmer next to a rock, on which the date June 20, 1863, is engraved. This recalls the date of admission to the Union. Above the arms is a ribbon with the text: "State of West Virginia."

Capital: Charleston
Area (sq. km): 62,384
Population: 1,850,000

Wisconsin

The Badger State

Wisconsin is one of the 26 states, which have a blue flag with the state's coat of arms. It was first adopted on April 29, 1913. As it looked like many other state flags, the name of the state and the date of admission to the Union were added on May 1, 1981. Governor Nelson Dewey designed the arms in 1851, while he was sitting on the steps of a New York bank. The crest is a badger, referring to the state's nickname.

Capital: Madison
Area (sq. km): 140,672
Population: 5,300,000

Wyoming

The Equality State

Miss Verna Keayes won the flag design competition, organized by the "Daughters of the American Revolution" in 1916. The red border represents the native Americans who owned the land before the settlers arrived. The blue represents the blue skies of Wyoming. White stands for purity and uprightness. The bison was once the monarch of the plains; the state seal was placed on him to represent the custom of branding. The flag is official since January 31, 1917.

Capital: Cheyenne
Area (sq. km): 251,501
Population: 490,000

Washington DC

Washington DC is neither a state nor a city. Its flag was adopted on October 15, 1938, by a special Congress commission. The flag of Washington DC is the banner of the coat of arms of George Washington's family, who lived in Sulgrave in the English county of Northampton. The arms were confirmed in 1592 to Laurence Washington. Red fringe was made an optional accessory for the Washington DC flag.

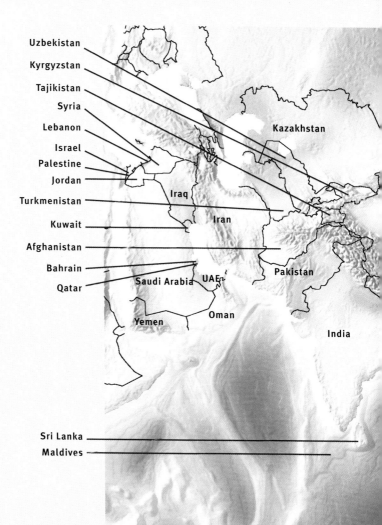

ASIA

Uzbekistan
Kyrgyzstan
Tajikistan
Syria
Lebanon
Israel
Palestine
Jordan
Turkmenistan
Kuwait
Afghanistan
Bahrain
Qatar

Kazakhstan

Iraq
Iran
Saudi Arabia   UAE
Yemen   Oman
Pakistan
India

Sri Lanka
Maldives

UAE = United Arab Emirates

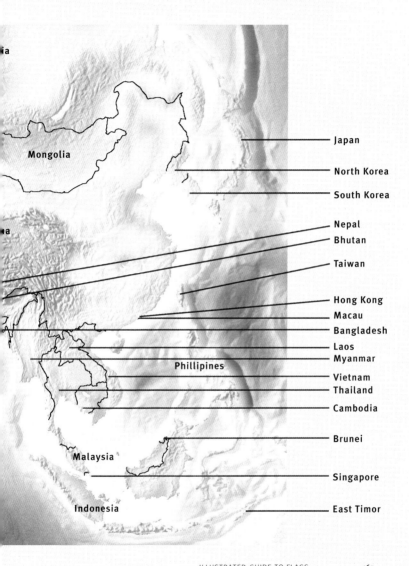

ia

Mongolia

ia

Japan

North Korea

South Korea

Nepal
Bhutan

Taiwan

Hong Kong
Macau
Bangladesh
Laos
Myanmar

Phillipines

Vietnam
Thailand
Cambodia

Brunei

Malaysia

Singapore

Indonesia

East Timor

More than half the world's population lives in ASIA, but these billions of people fly only 47 different national flags. The majority of flags hoisted and flown are from China and India, who together house one third of the people of the world.

Most modern Asian countries were born in the 20th century. Except for China and Japan, these countries were, for differing periods, ruled by other powers such as Turkey, Russia, the United Kingdom, The Netherlands, France, and the United States. The flags of these colonizers hardly influenced the flags of the Asian nations as we know them today. In the case of Malaysia, however, the American Stars and Stripes was copied in a way to display how many states the federation has.

The national flags of the Asian states are mainly based on religious symbolism. Most countries with a Muslim majority use Islamic colors and symbols in their flags. Pakistan, Maldives, Malaysia, Singapore, and Turkmenistan, for example, have their flags charged with a crescent and star. In addition, every Asian flag which shows the color green (even the flags of India and Sri Lanka) refers to the prophet Mohammad. Green also symbolizes hope and vegetation; to make something grow in the desert is an act of hard labor and a lot of hope.

In the Middle East, a number of countries have flags in the pan-Arab colors—red, green, white, and black. In the beginning of the 20th century, all these countries were part of the Ottoman Empire whose center was Turkey. In 1916, the Arabs revolted against the Turks and flew red, green, white, and black flags to show they wanted freedom. The Turks were among the losers

A parade celebrates the marriage of Crown Prince Naruhito and Crown Princess Masak of Japan.

of World War I, and their former territory in the Middle East was divided between the French and the British. In 1948, the state of Israel was established on Arab territory. The Jewish state adopted the Zionist flag with the Shield of David as the national flag, thus giving Asia another flag with a religious meaning.

Hinduism and Buddhism are other major eastern religions that are symbolized in some national flags. The colors of the flags of Nepal, Bhutan, and Sri Lanka reveal that Buddhism is important to them. That Hinduism is important in India is recalled in the use of orange stripe in its flag.

Socialism may be considered by some states in the Far East as a kind of religion. China, Vietnam, North Korea, and Laos have embraced this ideology, which they reveal in their flags by using the color red or by big stars. Countries that have abolished socialism or communism as the state ideology have recently changed their national symbols. Mongolia dropped its big yellow star, which expressed the union of the social classes. Cambodia returned to the flag under which it became independent.

When socialism collapsed in the Soviet Union in 1991, the federation fell apart into 15 new parts, five of them to be found in Central Asia. Their red Soviet-style banners were changed into multicolored flags. These were all designed from scratch, as none of them had any historic tradition. Where they felt Islam was important to them, they included crescents and the color green. Where they felt they were a Turkish people, they made use of the color blue, the traditional color of the Turkish people.

In the Far East, the color combination red and white is often seen, sometimes in conjunction with blue or yellow. These traditional colors have been used for centuries. Red very often is associated with blood. This color unifies mankind, as everybody has the same color blood. White is often related to purity of thought or ideals. It is striking that many flags in the Far East are charged with suns, moons, and stars. The sun brings light and happiness, stars lead the way, and moons express growth. Japan, the Land of the Rising Sun, has probably the simplest flag of the world.

Afghanistan

After more than two decades of civil war, the Interim Authority of Afghanistan, which was installed under UN supervision, came into power in December 2001. On January 26, 2002, this Authority readopted the flag in use before the outbreak of war. Black represents the 19th-century period when Afghanistan was occupied, red marks the struggle for independence, and green expresses hope for a prosperous future.

Capital: Kabul
Area (sq. km): 652,000
Population: 26,000,000
Languages: Dari, Pushtu
Currency: Afghani

Bahrain

Kingdom of Bahrain

The Arabs in the Gulf used plain red flags until they signed a treaty with Britain in 1820. In order to show they had peaceful intentions, all Arab states added a white stripe in their flags. Bahrain became independent on December 16, 1971, and its stripe was serrated. When it became a kingdom on February 14, 2002, the number of "teeth" in the serration was altered to five, to represent the pillars of Islam.

Capital: Manama
Area (sq. km): 675
Population: 635,000
Languages: Arabic, English
Currency: Bahraini Dinar

Bangladesh

People's Republic of Bangladesh

Bangladesh was a province of Pakistan until it broke away on March 26, 1971. The flag at that time was the same as today, but showed the map of the country on the red disk. This map was omitted on January 25, 1972. Green represents the country and the faith of the people—Islam has been declared the state religion. The red disc, which is set slightly toward the hoist, represents the struggle for independence.

Capital: Dakha
Area (sq. km): 144,000
Population: 130,000,000
Languages: Bengali, English
Currency: Taka

Bhutan

Kingdom of Bhutan

The upper-yellow triangle in Bhutan's flag signifies the secular authority of the King. Yellow is the color of fruitful action, in the affairs of religion as well as in state affairs. The orange lower triangle reflects Buddhism. The dragon recalls the people's name of their country: Druk Yul (the Land of the Thunder Dragon). The jewels in the dragon's claws are symbols of the land's wealth and perfection.

Capital: Thimphu
Area (sq. km): 47,000
Population: 785,000
Languages: Dzongkha, Nepali, English
Currency: Ngultrum

Brunei

Brunei Darussalam

The flag of Brunei has been in use since 1906, when the country became a British-protected state. After promulgation of the country's first constitution on September 29, 1959, the crest was added. This flag remained unchanged when Brunei became independent on January 1, 1984. Yellow is the color of the Sultan. The black and white stripes represent Brunei's main ministers (wazirs) who signed the 1906 Treaty.

Capital: Bandar Seri Begawan
Area (sq. km): 5,765
Population: 350,000
Languages: Malay, English
Currency: Brunei Dollar

Cambodia

Kingdom of Cambodia

Cambodia became independent from France on November 9, 1953. It had already established its flag five years earlier. Between 1970, when the country became involved in the Vietnam War, and 1993 the country has seen several flags. All contained the Angkor Wat, the ancient temple site built in the 12th century. The 1948 flag was reinstalled on June 29, 1993. Red and blue are traditional colors.

Capital: Phnom Penh
Area (sq. km): 181,000
Population: 12,000,000
Languages: Khmer, French, Chinese
Currency: Riel

China

People's Republic of China

The Chinese flag was adopted on October
1, 1949. Red symbolizes the Communist
Revolution, but reflects the Chinese
people as well as red is their traditional
color. The large yellow star stands for
the Communist Party. The four small
stars stand for the four social classes:
workers, peasants, and the urban and
national bourgeoisie. Yellow represents
brightness and symbolizes the "yellow"
race.

Capital: Beijing
Area (sq. km): 9,600,000
Population: 1,300,000,000
Languages: Chinese, local languages
Currency: Renminbi Yuan

East Timor

Democratic Republic of Timor-Leste

The former Portuguese colony East Timor
was occupied by Indonesia in 1975 and
finally became independent on May 20,
2002. Its flag is modeled on the flag of
the Fretelin independence party. Red
recalls the struggle for national
liberation. The yellow triangle stands
for the traces of colonialism. Black is
the obscurantism that needs to be
overcome. The white star represents
peace.

Capital: Dili
Area (sq. km): 14,900
Population: 840,000
Languages: Bahasa Indonesia, Portuguese
Currency: US Dollar

Hong Kong

Hong Kong Special Administrative Region of China

The former British Crown colony, Hong Kong was handed back to China on July 1, 1997. It became a special administrative region of China, which is reflected in its flag, chosen in 1990. Red recalls the Chinese communist revolution. The central emblem is a bauhinia flower, a climbing orchid that flowers one day a year. Each of the five petals bears a red star, to copy the number on the Chinese flag.

Capital: (none listed)
Area (sq. km): 1,100
Population: 7,200,000
Languages: Chinese, English
Currency: Hong Kong Dollar

India

Republic of India

The Indian flag was first hoisted at independence on August 15, 1947. Only from the beginning of 2002 have the Indian people been allowed to fly their flag whenever they like. The flag expresses the hope that Hindus (saffron) and Muslims (green) will live together in peace (white). The blue Chakra wheel is a Buddhist spinning wheel and symbolizes eternity. The 24 spokes correspond with the 24 hours of the day.

Capital: New Delhi
Area (sq. km): 3,287,300
Population: 1,015,000,000
Languages: Hindi, English, local languages
Currency: Indian Rupee

Indonesia

Republic of Indonesia

The Indonesian bicolor, which is the same as the national flag of Monaco, is called "Sang Saka Merah Putih," the Elevated Red and White. It was first flown on August 17, 1945, when Indonesia declared independence from The Netherlands. The colors are based on a banner of the 13th century Empire of Majahapit. Red material represents the color of the human blood and white spiritual life.

Capital: Jakarta
Area (sq. km): 1,904,500
Population: 220,000,000
Languages: Bahasa Indonesia, local languages
Currency: Rupiah

Iran

Islamic Republic of Iran

Green, white, and red were traditional colors used in Persia, the former name of Iran. The flag in its current form was adopted on July 29, 1980, to commemorate the Islamic Revolution of the previous year. Each of the red and green stripes is fringed with the stylized phrase "Allah-o-Akbar" (God is Great). This is repeated 22 times as a reminder of the date on the Islamic calendar (Bahman 22, 1357) when the Islamic Revolution was achieved (February 11, 1979).

Capital: Tehran
Area (sq. km): 1,648,000
Population: 65,750,000
Languages: Farsi, Kurdish, Baluchi
Currency: Rial

Iraq

Republic of Iraq

On January 12, 1991, at the brink of the Gulf War, President Saddam Hussein added in green the words "Allah-o-Akbar" (God is Great) between the three stars on the white stripe of the national flag. This flag was created in July 1963 and uses the pan-Arab colors, which represent the qualities of the people following Islam. The three stars of its design express the original will to unite with Egypt and Syria.

Capital: Baghdad
Area (sq. km): 438,300
Population: 22,900,000
Languages: Arabic, Kurdish
Currency: Iraqi Dinar

Israel

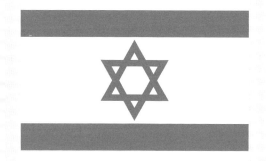

State of Israel

When Israel declared independence on May 14, 1948, it did not have a flag to hoist. Five months later, on October 28, the Provisional Council of State decided that the flag flown at the first Zionist Congress in Basle in 1897 should become the national flag. It was a creation of David Wolfsohn, who modeled it on the tallit, the Jewish prayer shawl. The star is the Shield of David, an ancient Jewish emblem.

Capital: Tel Aviv
Area (sq. km): 21,950
Population: 5,850,000
Languages: Hebrew, Arabic, English
Currency: Shekel

Japan

The Hinomaru (Rising Sun Flag) was only officially adopted as the national flag of Japan on August 13, 1999. Its history started in 1854 when ships were ordered to use a red disc on a white field as a flag. Japan is known as "The Land of the Rising Sun," symbolized in the flag with the red disc. It also represents sincerity, brightness, and warmth. The white field expresses purity and integrity.

Capital: Tokyo
Area (sq. km): 377,750
Population: 127,000,000
Languages: Japanese
Currency: Yen

Jordan

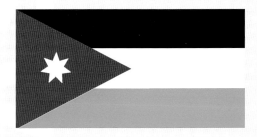

Hashemite Kingdom of Jordan

The Jordanian flag uses pan-Arab colors. It was established on April 16, 1928, when Jordan obtained nominal independence from the United Kingdom. Full independence was achieved on May 25, 1946. The black, white, and green stripes represent the Arab Abbasid, Umayyad, and Fatimid dynasties, while the red triangle symbolizes the Hashimite dynasty. The seven-pointed star stands for unity.

Capital: Amman
Area (sq. km): 98,000
Population: 6,350,000
Languages: Arabic
Currency: Jordanian Dinar

Kazakhstan

Republic of Kazakhstan

Kazakhstan gained independence on December 16, 1991, with the collapse of the Soviet Union. The flag was adopted on June 4, 1992. The sun in the blue field, which is the traditional color of the Turkic people, symbolizes the skies over the country. The flag's hoist is decorated with the traditional national ornament. Under the sun soars a berkut, a steppe eagle, which watches over freedom.

Capital: Astana
Area (sq. km): 2,717,300
Population: 15,500,000
Languages: Kazakh, Russian
Currency: Tenge

Korea (North)

Democratic People's Republic of Korea

The North Korean flag was adopted on September 9, 1948, when the country became an independent communist state. Blue, white, and red are traditional Korean colors. In the communist ideology, red represents the communist revolution expressed by the red star in the central stripe. The upper and lower blue stripes symbolize sovereignty, friendship, and peace. Purity is expressed by the white stripe.

Capital: Pyongyang
Area (sq. km): 120,550
Population: 23,500,000
Languages: Korean
Currency: Won

Korea (South)

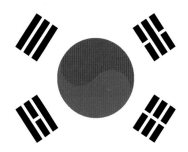

Republic of Korea

The South Korean flag was used by the Kingdom of Korea before 1910 and was adopted on September 8, 1948. In the center is the red and blue ying-yang symbol, which symbolizes the union of the opposites, such as man and woman, heaven and earth. The bar emblems in the four corners represent the elements of heaven, earth, water, and fire. White, representing purity, is a traditional color of the Korean people.

Capital: Seoul
Area (sq. km): 99,250
Population: 47,500,000
Languages: Korean
Currency: Won

Kuwait

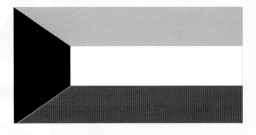

State of Kuwait

At independence from the United Kingdom on June 19, 1961, Kuwait used a red flag with its name in Arabic placed on it. This was changed to the current design on September 7, the same year. The flag is modeled on the 1916 Arab Revolt flag. Green represents fertility, white recalls purity, and red symbolizes the blood of the enemy on the Kuwaiti swords. The black trapezium symbolizes the defeat of the enemy.

Capital: Kuwait
Area (sq. km): 17,800
Population: 1,950,000
Languages: Arabic, English
Currency: Kuwaiti Dinar

Kyrgyzstan

Kyrgyz Republic

Kyrgyzstan declared its independence from the Soviet Union on August 31, 1991, when it flew a Soviet-styled flag. The current flag was adopted on March 3, 1992. Its red field recalls Manas, the ancient national hero who brought 40 tribes together to form the Kyrgyz nation. These tribes are recalled in the 40 sunrays. The sun emblem shows a stylized bird's-eye view of a yurt, the traditional tent which is used by the steppe people.

Capital: Bishkek
Area (sq. km): 198,500
Population: 4,875,000
Languages: Kyrgyz, Russian
Currency: Som

Laos

Lao People's Democratic Republic

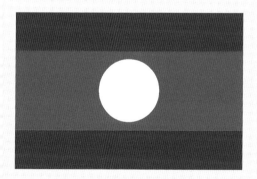

When Laos became a communist people's republic on December 2, 1975, the current flag was introduced. The red stripes at the top and bottom symbolize the blood shed in the struggle for independence from France, which was gained on October 23, 1975. The blue middle stripe stands for wealth, while the white disc is the full moon over the Mekong River. It also recalls unity under communism.

Capital: Vientiane
Area (sq. km): 236,800
Population: 5,500,000
Languages: Lao, French, English
Currency: Kip

Lebanon

Lebanese Republic

Before independence on November 22, 1943, Lebanon was a French Mandate. It used a French flag with a local cedar tree in the central stripe, representing holiness. On December 7, 1943, the current flag was adopted. The central white stripe is charged with a green cedar tree, the top and roots of which are touching the red stripes. The red stripes represent the blood shed for independence and white signifies purity.

Capital: Beirut
Area (sq. km): 10,400
Population: 4,275,000
Languages: Arabic, French, English
Currency: Lebanese Pound

Macau

Macau Special Administrative Region of China

The former Portuguese territory of Macau was handed over to China on December 20, 1999. Its flag, which was established in March 31, 1993, reflects its status as Special Administrative Region of China. The five yellow stars recall the fact Macau is part of China. The lotus symbolizes the Macau people. Its three petals stand for the Macau peninsula and its two islands. The bridge and waves symbolize the environment.

Capital: Macau
Area (sq. km): 18
Population: 475,000
Languages: Chinese, Portuguese
Currency: Pataca

Malaysia

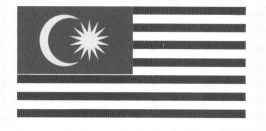

The Malaysian flag, first introduced in April 1950, is adapted from the Stars and Stripes. In its current form with 14 stripes, it was introduced on September 16, 1963. Every stripe and rays of the star represents a state, which is part of the federation. Since Singapore seceded in 1965, the 14th stripe represents the federal districts. The blue canton symbolizes unity of the Malay people. The crescent and star recall Islam.

Capital: Kuala Lumpur
Area (sq km): 329,750
Population: 22,500,000
Languages: Bahasa Malaysia, English
Currency: Malaysian Dollar

Maldives

Republic of Maldives

The Maldives, an archipelago consisting of more than 2,000 islands in the Indian Ocean, achieved independence from Britain on July 26, 1965. The Maldives flag, in its current form, was adopted on September 26 of the same year. The green panel symbolizes life, progress, and prosperity. The white crescent denotes the Islamic faith of the nation. The red borders recall the blood sacrificed in the struggle for national independence.

Capital: Male
Area (sq. km): 300
Population: 310,000
Languages: Dhivehi, Arabic, English
Currency: Rufiyaa

Mongolia

Mongolia was created on November 18, 1911, as the communist state of Outer Mongolia. Its flag dates from June 30, 1940, but until February 12, 1992, it had a communist yellow star in the hoist. The red stripes originally represented communism, but after 1992 they stand for progress. Light blue symbolizes the eternal sky. The yellow emblem is a soyombo, which combines several Buddhist elements.

Capital: Ulan Bator
Area (sq. km): 1,565,000
Population: 2,500,000
Languages: Khalkha Mongolian, Chinese, Russian
Currency: Tugrik

Myanmar

Union of Myanmar

Myanmar became independent from Britain as Burma on January 4, 1948. The country changed to its current name in 1989. The flag was adopted on January 4, 1974, to represent the new socialist ideology. The red field stands for courage, blue is for peace, and white represents purity. The 14 stars in the emblem represent the member states of the union. The cogwheel symbolizes industry and the rice is for agriculture.

Capital: Rangoon
Area (sq. km): 676,600
Population: 45,500,000
Languages: Burmese, English
Currency: Kyat

Nepal

Kingdom of Nepal

The Himalayan kingdom of Nepal is the only country in the world with a flag which is neither rectangular nor square. It consists of two triangles, which symbolize the peaks of the Himalayan range. It was adopted on December 16, 1962. The blue border represents peace. Red is the color of the rhododendron, the national flower of the kingdom; the moon represents the royal family, the sun symbolizes the Rana family.

Capital: Kathmandu
Area (sq. km): 147,200
Population: 24,750,000
Languages: Nepali
Currency: Nepalese Rupee

Oman

Sultanate of Oman

The flag of Oman in its current form was first flown on April 25, 1995, when the red middle stripe became the same width as the top and bottom stripes. White symbolizes peace and prosperity. Red, which is dominant, recalls the battles fought by Omanis through their history. The green stripe represents vegetation and fertility of the country. The dagger and crossed swords represent peace, defense, and justice.

Capital: Muscat
Area (sq. km): 212,500
Population: 2,500,000
Languages: Arabic
Currency: Omani Rial

Pakistan

Islamic Republic of Pakistan

The Muslim part of British India became
independent on August 14, 1947. The
flag was designed by Muhammed Ali
Jinnah, the founder of Pakistan. It is
basically the flag of the All-India Muslim
League, enhanced with a white stripe.
The crescent represents progress and
the star symbolizes knowledge. Green
is for Islam, and white represents the
country's non-Muslim groups.

Capital: Islamabad
Area (sq. km): 796,100
Population: 142,000,000
Languages: Punjabi, Sindi, Pushto, English
Currency: Pakistan Rupee

Palestine

Palestinian National Authority

Palestine comprises the West Bank of
Jordan and the Gaza Strip and is
occupied by Israel. It was not until May
18, 1994, that the Palestinian flag was
tolerated by Israel. The Palestinian flag,
which is also the flag of the Palestinian
Liberation Organization, dates from
1922 and it is similar to the Jordanian
national flag. Black, white, green, and
red are the pan-Arab colors.

Capital: East Jerusalem (claim)
Area (sq. km): 6,200
Population: 2,900,000
Languages: Arabic, English
Currency: Israeli Shekel

Philippines

Republic of the Philippines

The Philippines were still Spanish in 1897
when General Aguinaldo designed the
Filipino flag in exile. A year later, the
islands were ceded to the USA who
granted independence on July 4, 1946.
The white triangle represents equality.
The blue field stands for justice and the
red for patriotism. The sun recalls the
eight provinces, which started the
revolt against Spain. The three stars
represent the main islands.
Capital: Manila
Area (sq. km): 300,000
Population: 81,000,000
Languages: Filipino (Tagalog), English,
Spanish
Currency: Philippine Peso

Qatar

State of Qatar

To prove to the British that they had
peaceful intentions, nine Arab states
added white stripes to their red flags in
1820. The Gulf state of Qatar became
independent on September 1, 1971, but
had adopted the current flag in 1960.
Dark red (maroon), the color of clotted
blood, refers to blood spilled during
long wars and white stands for peace.
The nine "teeth" recall the nine Arab
states, which signed the 1820 Treaty.
Capital: Doha
Area (sq. km): 11,500
Population: 760,000
Languages: Arabic
Currency: Qatar Riyal

Saudi Arabia

Kingdom of Saudi Arabia

The prophet Muhammad was born in Mecca, which is in Saudi Arabia. The country was unified in 1927 and its current flag was adopted in 1973. The green field bears the Arabic inscription "There is no God but Allah, and Muhammad is the Prophet of Allah," (read from the right to the left). The sword, an ancient symbol of power, symbolizes justice.

Capital: Riyadh
Area (sq. km): 2,150,000
Population: 22,000,000
Languages: Arabic
Currency: Saudi Riyal

Singapore

Republic of Singapore

Singapore was part of Malaysia between September 16, 1963, and August 9, 1965, when it declared its independence. The flag was first hoisted on December 3, 1959. The red stripe symbolizes the brotherhood and equality of man, as everyone has red blood. White stands for purity. The crescent represents a young country whose ideals are represented by the five stars: democracy, peace, progress, justice, and equality.

Capital: Singapore
Area (sq. km): 660
Population: 4,050,000
Languages: Malay, English
Currency: Singapore Dollar

Sri Lanka

Democratic Socialist Republic of Sri Lanka

Ceylon was renamed Sri Lanka on May 22, 1972. On this occasion the current flag was first displayed. It differed slightly from the design introduced just after independence on February 4, 1948. The four leaves, which surround the lion, changed to Bo leaves which are Buddhist symbols. The lion flag was in use before the island became British in 1815. Yellow symbolizes the Buddhists, orange the Hindu, and green the Muslim populations.

Capital: Colombo
Area (sq. km): 65,600
Population: 19,300,000
Languages: Sinhali, Tamil, English
Currency: Sri Lankan Rupee

Syria

Syrian Arab Republic

Syria's flag is made of the pan-Arab colors red, white, green, and black. The country obtained its independence from France on April 12, 1946, and has since seen several flags, all expressing the actual political situation. The current flag was adopted on March 30, 1980, after Syria had ceded the union with Egypt and was planning a federation with Libya. The two stars refer to the proposed federation, which never materialized.

Capital: Damascus
Area (sq. km): 185,200
Population: 16,350,000
Languages: Arab, English
Currency: Syrian Pound

Taiwan

Republic of China

The flag of Taiwan was adopted on October 28, 1928, as the flag of the Republic of China. However, the communist Chinese expelled the nationalists with their flag, from the mainland to the island of Formosa in 1949. The blue canton shows the original Kuomingtang Party flag. The sun has 12 rays; each represents two hours of the day. The red field symbolizes the Chinese people, as this is their traditional color.

Capital: Taipei
Area (sq. km): 35,750
Population: 22,280,000
Languages: Mandarin, Taiwanese
Currency: New Taiwan Dollar

Tajikistan

Republic of Tajikistan

Tajikistan declared its independence from the Soviet Union on September 9, 1991, just before this Union dissolved into 15 parts. Its red Soviet-styled flag was changed to the current one on November 24, 1992. The country's name is derived from "tajvar," which means crowned. In the flag, the crown symbolizes the Tajik people. The seven stars shine for perfectionism. White stands for purity, green for Islam, and red for victory.

Capital: Dushanbe
Area (sq. km): 143,100
Population: 6,250,000
Languages: Tajik, Russian
Currency: Somoni

Thailand

Kingdom of Thailand

It is impossible to fly the Thai Trairanga (tricolour) upside down. That was the first requisite of King Rami VI, when he decided on September 28, 1917, to change the country's flag. By choosing the colors red, white, and blue, the king expressed his solidarity with the World War I allies (US, UK, Russia, and France). Red symbolized blood shed for the country, white is the purity of Buddhism, and blue stands for the monarchy.

Capital: Bangkok
Area (sq. km): 514,000
Population: 61,500,000
Languages: Thai, Malay, English
Currency: Baht

Turkmenistan

Turkmenistan broke away from the Soviet Union on October 27, 1991. Its flag was adopted on February 19, 1992. At the hoist is a carpet design showing medallions or guls of the tribes who wove the famous Turkmen carpets. In 1997, the UN emblem was added to symbolize the policy of neutrality. The green field and crescent moon represent Islam and the five stars are the traditional Turkmen regions.

Capital: Ashgabat
Area (sq. km): 488,100
Population: 4,600,000
Languages: Turkmen, Russian
Currency: Manat

United Arab Emirates

The United Arab Emirates consist of seven emirates, which merged to become independent from Britain on December 2, 1971. On that date the flag, which is made of the pan-Arab colors, was first hoisted. The red stripe at the hoist recalls the historical flags of the emirates, which all were plain red. The green stripe symbolizes fertility of the land, the white stripe expresses neutrality, and the black one symbolizes the rich oil fields.

Capital: Abu Dhabi
Area (sq. km): 77,700
Population: 2,400,000
Languages: Arabic, English
Currency: UAE Dirham

Uzbekistan

Republic of Uzbekistan

Uzbekistan broke away from the Soviet Union on August 31, 1991. It changed its Soviet-style red flag for the current one on November 18, that same year. The blue stripe represents the sky and water, white stands for peace, and the green stripe symbolizes nature and vegetation. The small red stripes indicate the will to survive and the crescent shows the people's will to develop. The months of the year are represented by stars.

Capital: Tashkent
Area (sq. km): 447,400
Population: 24,750,000
Languages: Uzbek, Russian
Currency: Sum

Vietnam

Socialist Republic of Vietnam

After the French withdrawal in 1954, Vietnam became an ideologically divided country. The communist North and the capitalist South each adopted its own flag. When North and South Vietnam merged in 1976, the reunified country adopted the flag that North Vietnam had used since November 30, 1955. The communist red also recalls the blood spilled for independence. The yellow star symbolizes the cooperation of the classes.

Capital: Hanoi
Area (sq. km): 331,100
Population: 78,000,000
Languages: Vietnamese, French, English
Currency: Dong

Yemen

Republic of Yemen

Yemen is the product of the unification of North and South Yemen on May 22, 1990. The flag, in the pan-Arab colors, is based on the flags that North and South Yemen used before merging. Both flags were charged with stars, in different colors, which symbolized different ideologies. The current flag's meaning is: two countries were born by revolution (red), were reunited in peace (white), and will remember their dark past (black).

Capital: Sanaa
Area (sq. km): 528,000
Population: 17,500,000
Languages: Arabic
Currency: Riyal

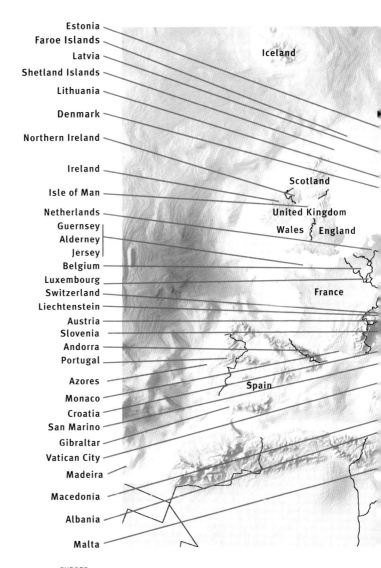

Estonia

Faroe Islands

Latvia

Shetland Islands

Lithuania

Denmark

Northern Ireland

Ireland

Isle of Man

Netherlands

Guernsey

Alderney

Jersey

Belgium

Luxembourg

Switzerland

Liechtenstein

Austria

Slovenia

Andorra

Portugal

Azores

Monaco

Croatia

San Marino

Gibraltar

Vatican City

Madeira

Macedonia

Albania

Malta

Iceland

Scotland

United Kingdom

Wales England

France

Spain

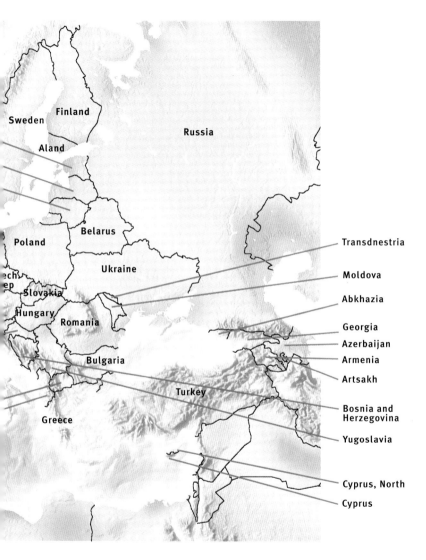

Sweden

Finland

Aland

Russia

Poland

Belarus

Ukraine

ech
ep

Slovakia

Hungary

Romania

Transdnestria

Moldova

Abkhazia

Georgia

Azerbaijan

Armenia

Artsakh

Bulgaria

Turkey

Greece

Bosnia and
Herzegovina

Yugoslavia

Cyprus, North

Cyprus

In terms of culture and civilization, EUROPE is seen as the oldest continent and accordingly, one can find the world's oldest flags here. In the Middle Ages, Europe's wealth was earned by exploration and ships sailed around the globe using flags to signal and to let other ships know were they came from. This use of pieces of cloth, flying in ships as signs of identification, was the beginning of the development of flags as we know them today.

The older a flag is, the less we know about its origin and symbolic meaning. Denmark claims to hold the world record. The Danes cultivate the legend that in 1219 God signaled them with their current flag on the battlefield. They saw this as a sign that God approved of their efforts to convert heathens into Christians. True or not, what is certain is that the official design of the Dannebrog, as the Danes call their national flag, was first legally described in 1625. This was more than 25 years after the Swedes had described their flag as a naval ensign. The Swedes do not claim they hold the record for the world's oldest flag, because they admit theirs was modeled on that of Denmark.

Does The Netherlands, then, have the world's oldest flag? It was first used in rebel ships at the beginning of the War of Independence against Spain in 1572. Some decades later however, the Dutch altered the upper stripe from its original orange color to red, the reason being lost to history.

The British Union Flag took its current design in 1801, when Ireland's entry into the Union was represented by an extra cross. Its original form was created in 1606 when James I acceded to the English throne. One thing is certain, that the Union Flag provided the colors of the American Stars and

Fans wave Norwegian flags at the 1994 Winter Olympic Games in Lillehammer, Norway.

Stripes. The Union Flag was later copied in other flags and miniature versions can still be found in other flags, such as those of Australia and New Zealand.

All other Western European flags are relatively young inventions. Among them is the French blue, white, and red flag, La Tricolore, or tricolor that has influenced many other flags of the world. When it was established at the time of the French Revolution, it was seen worldwide as a revolutionary sign. Under this flag, the French were able to create new human relations, so it expressed the will to do the same around the world. Every continent has at least one flag that is modeled on the French flag. Even Norway honors the French flag by the use of the same colors.

The French Revolution triggered the birth of countries such as Italy and Germany. Both countries were collections of feudal states where people spoke the same languages. Their flags were born at the beginning of the process of unity.

Russia's flag only came into use at the end of the 17th century, when the country built up a navy and needed signs for identification. A century and a half later, Russia constituted itself as protector of the Slav people, who were part of the Austrian-Hungarian or Ottoman Empires and longed for freedom. The oppressed Slavs had no flags of their own, so they copied the Russian colors and put them in a different order. This may still be seen in the national flags of countries such as Croatia, Slovakia, and Bulgaria.

After World War I, Europe saw an increase in the number of independent flag-flying states. New countries, such as Poland, Czechoslovakia, and Yugoslavia were created. Some other new states were annexed by the communist-ruled Soviet Union, the successor of the Russian Empire. After World War II, the Soviet Union spread its influence over Europe. At the end of the 1980s, its power declined and the multi-ethnic nations, including the Soviet Union, Yugoslavia, and Czechoslovakia, disintegrated. This was the last boom in European national flags. Some of the new nations celebrated their newfound independence by readopting flags they had used in earlier days, while others were newly invented.

In building toward a united Europe, the member states of the European Union have adopted the blue EU flag as their second flag. Non-member states also use it to express their desire to remain connected with the rest of Europe. The European flag, however, is not seen as a substitute for national flags.

Abkhazia

Republic of Abkhazia (Apsny)

Valeri Gamgia's design for Abkhazia's flag was adopted on July 23, 1992, when the territory broke with Georgia in the Caucasus. The seven stripes express that Muslims (green) can live in peace with Christians (white). The open hand on a red field is taken from a 14th century map, which showed this as the flag for Abkhazia. The seven stars are the historical districts.

Capital: Sukhumi
Area (sq. km): 8,600
Population: 560,000
Languages: Abkhazian, Georgian, Russian
Currency: Russian Rouble

Åland

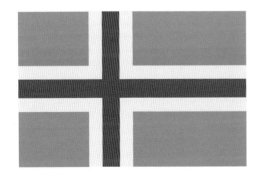

Åland Island

Åland consists of 6,500 islands between Finland and Sweden. Although the people in the islands are Swedish speaking, they were not permitted to merge with Sweden in 1921, but were granted autonomy by Finland. In their flag—approved by the Finnish president on March 31, 1954—they express their Swedish heritage. It is basically a Swedish flag charged with an extra red cross to symbolize Finland.

Capital: Mariehamn
Area (sq. km): 6,800
Population: 26,000
Languages: Swedish, Finnish
Currency: Euro

Albania

Republic of Albania

Albania declared its independence from the Ottoman Empire on November 28, 1912, when the red flag with the double-headed eagle was first flown. In Albanian, the country's name means "Land of the Eagle." The eagle had been an Albanian emblem since the 15th century. From 1944 to 1991, when the country was a strict communist state, the flag was charged with a communist red star.

Capital: Tirana
Area (sq. km): 28,750
Population: 3,500,000
Languages: Albanian
Currency: Lek

Andorra

Principality of Andorra

The flag of Andorra is based on the flags of France and Spain, the two states that protect the independence of the miniature state on the tops of the Pyrenees. The design of vertical bars is taken from the French Tricolore, as is the blue and red. Yellow and red are taken from the Spanish and Catalan flags. The motto in the coat of arms "Virtus Unita Fortior," means "Strength United is Stronger."

Capital: Andorra la Vella
Area (sq. km): 470
Population: 67,000
Languages: Catalan, Spanish, French
Currency: Euro

Armenia

Republic of Armenia

Armenia was a Soviet republic from 1922 until September 21, 1991, when it declared independence. The flag dates from between 1918 and 1920 when the country was briefly independent. It was readopted on August 24, 1990, anticipating renewed autonomy. The red stripe recalls the blood shed for independence, the blue stands for hope and the Armenian skies. Orange symbolizes Armenian courage.

Capital: Yerevan
Area (sq. km): 29,800
Population: 3,800,000
Languages: Armenian, Russian
Currency: Dram

Artsakh

Republic of Nagory-Karabach

Artsakh is politically part of Islamic Azerbaijan, but has a Christian Armenian population. At the fall of the Soviet Union, Artsakh declared unilateral independence on December 10, 1991. Its flag, adopted on July 3, 1992, is based on the Armenian flag, expressing their wish to merge with the country seen as their home. That Artsakh is separated from its homeland is symbolized by the white ravel cut in the flags fly.

Capital: Stepanakert
Area (sq. km): 4,400
Population: 155,000
Languages: Armenian, Russian
Currency: Armenian Dram

Austria

Republic of Austria

The Austrians say that during the Middle Ages there was a Duke who fought so fiercely in battle that his white coat was soaked in blood. When he took off his sword belt, a white stripe was left on his coat, providing the inspiration for their flag. Probably just a tale, but Austria's colors are among the oldest in the world. The flag was adopted after the fall of the Habsburg Dynasty in 1918. Between 1938 and 1945 Austria, as part of Nazi Germany, flew the swastika flag.

Capital: Vienna
Area (sq. km): 83,900
Population: 8,200,000
Languages: German
Currency: Euro

Azerbaijan

Azerbaijani Republic

After a brief period of independence between 1918 and 1920, Azerbaijan became part of the Soviet Union until it seceded on October 18, 1991. On February 5, 1991, parliament had readopted the flag that had flown during the first independence. The colors mean that Azerbaijan is ready to Turkify (blue), Islamisize (green and the crescent), and Europeanize (red). The eight-star points represent all Turkish people.

Capital: Baku
Area (sq. km): 86,600
Population: 8,100,000
Languages: Azeri, Russian
Currency: Manat

Azores

Autonomous Region of the Azores

The Azores is an autonomous Portuguese archipelago in the Atlantic Ocean. Its flag was approved by the regional parliament on April 4, 1979. The colors are the same as the pre-1911 Portuguese flag. The alliance with the mother country is shown through the Portuguese arms in the canton. The hawk (açor) refers to the name of the country. The nine stars symbolize the nine islands, which make up the Azores.

Capital: Ponta Delgada
Area (sq. km): 2,300
Population: 240,000
Languages: Portuguese
Currency: Euro

Belarus

Republic of Belarus

Formally known as White Russia, Belarus declared independence from the Soviet Union on August 25, 1991. It adopted a white, red, white tricolor, which had been flying during a brief period of independence just after World War II. In 1994, Alexander Lukashenka was elected president. As he favored communism, he decreed that they should adopt a flag based on the flag White Russia used during its Soviet era.

Capital: Minsk
Area (sq. km): 207,600
Population: 10,400,000
Languages: Belarussian, Russian
Currency: Belarussian Rouble

Belgium

Kingdom of Belgium

Belgium declared its independence from The Netherlands in August 1830. Black, yellow, and red had previously been used as colors of freedom in 1792 during an attempt to declare independence from Austria which ruled Belgium at the time. As the 1792 flag had horizontal stripes, like the Dutch flag, the Belgians reversed the stripes vertically. It is an imitation of the French Tricolore to honor the French spirit of revolution and liberty.

Capital: Brussels
Area (sq. km): 30,500
Population: 10,500,000
Languages: Dutch, French, German
Currency: Euro

Bosnia and Herzegovina

The flag of Bosnia and Herzegovina was imposed by the European High Representative on February 4, 1998. He acts as a referee in the former Yugoslav republic which saw an ethnic war between 1992 and 1995. The design is strictly neutral. Dark blue and yellow refer to the European flag. The yellow triangle is a graphic interpretation of the country. The three sides recall the three ethnic groups: Muslims, Croats, and Serbs.

Capital: Sarajevo
Area (sq. km): 51,200
Population: 3,900,000
Languages: Bosnian, Serbian, Croat
Currency: Marka

Bulgaria

Republic of Bulgaria

The Bulgarian tricolor is based on the pan-Slav colors, but has changed blue for green. In its current form, the flag came into use on November 22, 1990, when, after the collapse of Marxism, the communist-styled coat of arms was omitted from the white stripe. The white stripe symbolizes love and peace. The green band represents the vitality of the nation, while the red stands for the valor of the people.

Capital: Sofia
Area (sq. km): 110,900
Population: 7,800,000
Languages: Bulgarian
Currency: Lev

Croatia

Republic of Croatia

Croatia declared its independence from Yugoslavia on June 25, 1991. The flag in the pan-Slav colors had been adopted on December 22, 1990, on the occasion of the promulgation of a new constitution. The center of the flag is charged with the Croat coat of arms, to avoid confusion with the Dutch flag. The red and white checks are traditional for Croatia. The crown consists of the shields of the five ancient Croat regions.

Capital: Zagreb
Area (sq. km): 56,500
Population: 4,500,000
Languages: Croatian
Currency: Kuna

Cyprus

Republic of Cyprus

Cyprus is the only country in the world with a map on its flag. It was first hoisted on August 16, 1960, when the island became independent from Britain. The flag is of a neutral design, as the Greek and Turkish people were heavily divided. The hope for peace between the two groups is illustrated by the two olive branches. The map of the island is copper yellow to illustrate the name of Cyprus—the Isle of Copper.

Capital: Nicosia
Area (sq. km): 9,250
Population: 760,000
Languages: Greek, Turkish
Currency: Cyprus Pound

Cyprus, North

Turkish Republic of Northern Cyprus

The northern part of Cyprus, traditionally inhabited by Turkish people, declared independence on November 15, 1983. The Turkish flag was hoisted to indicate that they wanted to join that country. The current flag, based on the flag of Turkey, was adopted on March 9, 1984, and reaffirms the country's independence. Turkey is the only country that has recognized Northern Cyprus' independence.

Capital: Lefkosa
Area (sq. km): 3,350
Population: 201,000
Languages: Turkish
Currency: Turkish Lira

Czech Republic

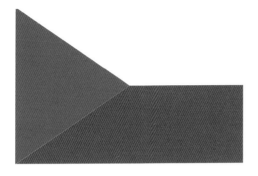

The Czech Republic and Slovakia split on January 1, 1993. They had been united as Czechoslovakia, in 1919, under one flag composed of the pan-Slav colors. That flag was taken over by the Czech Republic. White and red are the traditional colors of Bohemia, one region of the Czech Republic. The blue triangle symbolizes Moravia, the other part of the country.

Capital: Prague
Area (sq. km): 78,700
Population: 10,500,000
Languages: Czech
Currency: Koruna

Denmark

Kingdom of Denmark

The Danes are convinced their Dannebrog (Danish Cloth) is the oldest flag in the world. Legend has it that it appeared from heaven in 1219 as a sign from God that the Danes had done a good job converting the Estonians to Christianity. The Dannebrog, officially adopted in 1625, is copied by all of the other Scandinavian countries. Danish naval ships use the Dannebrog with a large cut at the fly in the shape of a swallowtail.

Capital: Copenhagen
Area (sq. km): 43,100
Population: 5,400,000
Languages: Danish
Currency: Danish Krone

Estonia

Republic of Estonia

The Estonian colors were chosen by a group of young intellectuals in 1881 as the symbol of the Estonian Students' Society. At the time, Estonia was under Tsarist rule. Between the two World Wars, Estonia was independent under these colors. Blue is the sky above the country. Black stands for the soil and the dark past. White represents purity. Anticipating a break with the Soviet Union, this flag was readopted on May 8, 1990.

Capital: Talinn
Area (sq. km): 45,100
Population: 1,450,000
Languages: Estonain, Russian
Currency: Kroon

Faroe Islands

Unlike Denmark, during World War II the Faroe Islands weren't occupied by Germany. Unable to fly the Danish flag, Faroese fishing boats started using Merkid (Sign), as their ensign is called. Designed in 1919 by Faroese students who favored autonomy, the Merkid was officially adopted in 1948 when this was achieved. Currently, the islands aim for independence.

Capital: Torshavn
Area (sq. km): 1,400
Population: 44,000
Languages: Faroes, Danish
Currency: Danish Krone

Finland

Republic of Finland

Finland was part of Tsarist Russia in 1861 when the Nyland Yacht Club was granted a special yacht ensign—a blue cross on a white field charged with the clubs badge. This ensign became a rallying symbol for independence, which was achieved on December 6, 1917. The Finnish say that the blue stands for Finland's thousands of lakes and beautiful sky and the white for the glittering snow cover of the winter.

Capital: Helsinki
Area (sq. km): 338,200
Population: 5,200,000
Languages: Finnish, Swedish
Currency: Euro

France

French Republic

The French Tricolore, as their flag is named, became a symbol of liberty all over the world. It substituted the royal white flag with the fleur-de-lis, or lily, on February 15, 1794, five years after the French Revolution. Blue and red are the city colors of Paris, where the flag was conceived. The white stripe originally expressed that the bourgeoisie (blue and red) were aiming for cooperation with the royals (white).

Capital: Paris
Area (sq km): 551,500
Population: 61,000,000
Languages: French, regional languages
Currency: Euro

Georgia

Republic of Georgia

The Caucasian republic of Georgia regained independence on April 9, 1991. After a brief period of independence between 1917 and 1921, it was absorbed by the Soviet Union. The current flag was introduced in that period of first independence. The main field is deep red, nearly brown, which is the traditional national color of Georgia. The black and white canton reveals that the country had a dark past, but its future is bright.

Capital: Tbilisi
Area (sq. km): 69,700
Population: 5,400,000
Languages: Georgian, Russian
Currency: Laria

Germany

Federal Republic of Germany

The black, red, and yellow were introduced as the flag when the country was first unified in 1848. These colors were introduced in 1813 by students who fought for a unified Germany. The country has seen several flag changes; during World War II, it flew the Swastika flag of the Nazis. After the war the country was divided into Eastern and Western states, which were reunited again in 1991 after the collapse of USSR.

Capital: Berlin
Area (sq. km): 357,000
Population: 83,000,000
Languages: German
Currency: Euro

Gibraltar

Gibraltar is a British dependency on the south coast of the Spanish mainland. Queen Elisabeth II approved the Gibraltar City flag in 1983, but it had already come into use at the beginning of the 20th century. It is based on the city arms, which were approved in 1502. The castle represents Gibraltar as a fortress, while the key indicates the city's important geographical position at the entrance to the Mediterranean Sea.

Capital: Gibraltar
Area (sq. km): 6
Population: 28,500
Languages: English
Currency: Gibraltar Pound

Greece

Hellenic Republic

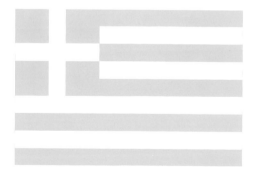

The Greek flag is based on the Stars and Stripes. It came into use at the beginning of the 19th century, when Greece was part of the Ottoman Empire. Blue symbolizes the Greek seas and skies. White represents the purity of the Greek struggle for independence, which was proclaimed on January 13, 1822, when the flag was adopted. The cross reflects the Greek Orthodox faith of the people.

Capital: Athens
Area (sq. km): 132,000
Population: 10,700,000
Languages: Greek
Currency: Euro

Hungary

Republic of Hungary

Until November 16, 1919, Hungary was part of the Austrian-Hungarian Empire. Flags in the colors red, white, and green first appeared in a major uprising in 1848–1849. Red symbolized strength, white faithfulness, and green hope for a prosperous future. After the World War II, the communist regime added socialist arms in the center of the flag. During the 1957 uprising the people cut this hated emblem out and flew flags with holes.

Capital: Budapest
Area (sq. km): 93,000
Population: 10,200,000
Languages: Hungarian
Currency: Forint

Iceland

Republic of Iceland

Iceland achieved full independence from Denmark on June 17, 1944. The island had obtained the right to fly a distinctive flag on November 22, 1913; the current flag, however, was not adopted until June 19, 1915. The design expresses that Iceland is part of the Nordic community. Blue and white are the traditional colors of Iceland. Red refers to Norway, where most of the Vikings who settled in Iceland came from.

Capital: Reykjavik
Area (sq. km): 103,000
Population: 275,000
Languages: Icelandic
Currency: Icelandic Krone

Ireland

Republic of Ireland

The Irish tricolor is modeled on that of the French and was introduced by Thomas Francis Meagher in the 1848 uprising against the British. The colors express the wish that Catholics (green) and Protestants (orange) will live together in peace (white). Ireland is called the Green Island and orange refers to William of Orange, who led the Protestant immigrants. Irish independence was achieved after the 1916 Easter Rising in 1921.

Capital: Dublin
Area (sq. km): 70,300
Population: 3,800,000
Languages: Irish, English
Currency: Euro

Italy

Italian Republic

It was not until 1861 that Italy was unified under the House of Savoy. The Italian tricolor, however, was first displayed as the national flag of the Cisalpine Republic on May 11, 1798. As France supported unification, the design is modeled on the French Tricolore. Until the monarchy was abolished after a referendum on June 18, 1946, the flag was charged with the coat of arms of the House of Savoy.

Capital: Rome
Area (sq. km): 301,300
Population: 57,800,000
Languages: Italian
Currency: Euro

Latvia

Republic of Latvia

Latvia achieved its independence on November 18, 1918, but was forced to become part of the Soviet Union in 1940. The flag originates from that first period of freedom and was based on a banner described in 1296. The flag symbolizes the readiness of the Latvians to give the blood of their heart for their freedom (white). It became Latvia's flag again on February 15, 1990, in anticipation of the break with the Soviet Union on August 21, 1991.

Capital: Riga
Area (sq. km): 64,600
Population: 2,900,000
Languages: Latvian, Russian
Currency: Lats

Liechtenstein

Principality of Liechtenstein

At the Berlin Olympic Games in 1936, Liechtenstein discovered it had the same flag as Haiti. The following year the prince of this tiny country, that nestles between Austria and Switzerland, decided to add a princely crown to the flag. Liechtenstein obtained its independence on July 12, 1806. Royal blue and red have been used as national colors ever since. When the flag is displayed vertically, the crown has to stay upright.

Capital: Vaduz
Area (sq. km): 160
Population: 33,000
Languages: German
Currency: Swiss Franc

Lithuania

Republic of Lithuania

On March 11, 1990, Lithuania became the
first Soviet Republic to declare its
independence. On November 18,1988, it
had also been the first Baltic state to
readopt the flag it flew during the
period of independence between World
War I and II. The tricolor was first
approved on April 19, 1918. Yellow,
green, and red are traditional
Lithuanian colors, which are used in
traditional national dress.

Capital: Vilnius
Area (sq. km): 65,200
Population: 3,750,000
Languages: Lithuanian, Russian
Currency: Litas

Luxembourg

Grand Duchy of Luxembourg

The Luxembourg flag is very similar to the
Dutch tricolor, but the shade of the
blue of the Luxembourg flag is much
paler. Although the Dutch royal family
owned the grand duchy until November
12, 1890, as part of The Netherlands,
the colors are the same by coincidence.
The Luxembourg colors date back to
the 13th century. The flag was only
officially adopted as the Luxembourg
tricolor on August 16, 1972.

Capital: Luxembourg
Area (sq. km): 2,600
Population: 440,000
Languages: French, German,
Luxembourgish
Currency: Euro

Macedonia

[Former Yugoslav] Republic of Macedonia

In order to obtain international recognition, the former Yugoslav Republic of Macedonia was forced to change its flag, which they did on October 5, 1995. After its declaration of independence on September 8, 1991, Macedonia adopted a red flag with the ancient Star of Vergina in the center. The Greek neighbors saw this as insulting so, to settle this conflict, Macedonia changed the star for a sun.

Capital: Skopje
Area (sq. km): 25,700
Population: 2,100,000
Languages: Macedonian, Albanian
Currency: Denar

Madeira

Autonomous Region of Madeira

Madeira is an autonomous Portuguese island in the Atlantic Ocean. Its flag was adopted by the regional parliament on July 28, 1978. The blue stripes symbolize the ocean, which surrounds the island (yellow stripe). The central cross of the Order of Christ, recalls Prince Henri the Navigator. During his reign, the islands were discovered in 1419 and colonized by Portuguese immigrants.

Capital: Funchal
Area (sq. km): 780
Population: 265,000
Languages: Portugues
Currency: Euro

Malta

Republic of Malta

The national colors of white and red where given to Malta in 1090 by Count Roger the Norman, who had landed on the island to oust the Arabs. The islands became a Christian stronghold during the Crusades. In World War II, Malta was awarded the George Cross for the heroism of its people and the honors were charged on the flag. Malta became independent from Britain on September 21, 1964, when the flag became official.

Capital: Valetta
Area (sq. km): 315
Population: 385,000
Languages: Maltese, English
Currency: Maltese Lira

Moldova

Republic of Moldova

In August 1940, the Soviet Union forced Romania to cede Moldova to form a Soviet republic. When the Soviet Union collapsed in 1991, Moldova decided not to reunite with Romania. Its flag, however (adopted on April 27, 1990), is based on that of Romania. In the center is the coat of arms, which shows the eagle of Walachia and the traditional shield of Moldavia.

Capital: Chisinau
Area (sq. km): 33,700
Population: 4,350,000
Languages: Romanian, Ukrainian, Russian
Currency: Moldovan Leu

Monaco

Principality of Monaco

The Monegasque flag was approved by Prince Charles on April 4, 1881. The tiny principality on the French Mediterranean coast heavily protested in 1945 when Indonesia adopted their red and white flag; however, they never received a reply from Jakarta. Today, the Grimalidi family rules the principality. Their family colors are red and white. When Monaco no longer has a prince successor, it will cede to France.

Capital: Monaco
Area (sq. km): 1.5
Population: 32,000
Languages: French
Currency: Euro

The Netherlands

Kingdom of the Netherlands

The first Dutch flag was orange, white, and blue and came into use during the 1568–1648 War of Independence. The blue and white colors expressed that Prince William of Orange supported freedom of religion. The orange stripe changed into red around 1620 and was made official on February 17, 1937. An orange streamer is flown with the flag at the birthdays of members of the Royal House of Orange.

Capital: Amsterdam
Area (sq. km): 41,500
Population: 16,100,000
Languages: Dutch
Currency: Euro

Norway

Kingdom of Norway

After being ruled by Denmark and Sweden, Norway became independent on October 27, 1905, when the union with Sweden dissolved. Its flag, however, originated from July 17, 1821 when Norway received a certain amount of autonomy. The flag is based on the Danish Dannebrog. The white cross was overlaid with a blue cross, which gave the flag the same colors as the French Tricolore. This was seen as a symbol of liberty.

Capital: Oslo
Area (sq. km): 323,900
Population: 4,500,000
Languages: Norwegian
Currency: Norwegian Krone

Poland

Republic of Poland

The Polish bicolor was adopted on August 1, 1919, by the provisional parliament. Independence was proclaimed the following November. White and red have been in use as Polish colors since the 13th century and were taken from the national arms. They show a white eagle on a red ground and date from 1228. The state flag shows the national coat of arms in the white stripe.

Capital: Warsaw
Area (sq. km): 323,250
Population: 39,000,000
Languages: Polish
Currency: Zloty

Portugal

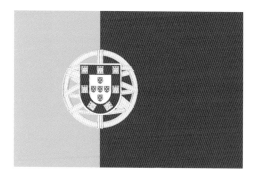

Portuguese Republic

Portugal became a republic on June 19, 1911, on which occasion the current flag was adopted. The red panel symbolizes revolution, while the green represents hope for a prosperous future. The flag is charged with an armillary sphere, an early navigation instrument. It refers to Henri the Navigator, under whose reign in the 15th century Portugal became a sea power. The armillary sphere is decorated with the national arms.

Capital: Lisbon
Area (sq. km): 92,300
Population: 10,100,000
Languages: Portuguese
Currency: Euro

Romania

Since December 27, 1989, when Romania abolished communism, it has had the same flag as the African country Chad. The Romanian flag was charged with the communist-styled coat of arms, but the angry people cut it away. Blue, yellow, and red were first used in the European Revolution Year, 1848. These are the traditional colors of the principalities of Moldavia and Wallachia, which became independent in 1859 as Romania.

Capital: Bucharest
Area (sq. km): 238,400
Population: 22,600,000
Languages: Romanian
Currency: Leu

Russia

Russian Federation

Since the Russian flag was first introduced in 1699 it has had a major influence on the flags of other East European countries and the colors became the pan-Slav colors. It was established when Russia was developing itself as a seafaring nation under Peter the Great. White, blue, and red were originally the colors of Moscow. From 1918 until August 22, 1991, when the current flag was readopted, Russia flew a red flag.

Capital: Moscow
Area (sq. km): 17,075,400
Population: 145,500,000
Languages: Russian, many local languages
Currency: Russian Rouble

San Marino

Republic of San Marino

Tiny San Marino is the world's oldest and smallest republic. Since 1599, a team of two presidents has been elected twice a year. The flag dates back to 1797 and was recognized by Napoleon in 1799 as that of an independent nation. White and blue are taken from the coat of arms, which were introduced in the 18th century. The flag is charged with these arms, which also show the motto "Libertas" (Liberty).

Capital: San Marino
Area (sq. km): 61
Population: 27,500
Languages: Italian
Currency: Euro

Slovakia

Slovak Republic

Slovakia was part of Czechoslovakia until January 1, 1993, when the Czech Republic and Slovakia separated. The Slovak flag, which was adopted on September 1, 1992, anticipating independence, is based on the pan-Slav colors. In order to distinguish it from the Russian flag, Slovakia charged it with the national coat of arms. This shows a red field with a white patriarchal cross on three blue (Slovakian) mountains.

Capital: Bratislava
Area (sq. km): 49,000
Population: 5,500,000
Languages: Slovak, Hungarian, Czech
Currency: Koruna

Slovenia

Republic of Slovenia

Two days before its breach with Yugoslavia on June 26, 1991, Slovenia adopted its current flag. As the Slovenians are a Slavic people, they are using the pan-Slav colors. In the canton is the coat of arms, which depicts Triglav, the highest mountain in the Slovenian Alps. The stars represent the former duchy of Celje. The country's name and flag are easily confused with those of Slovakia, so Slovenia is considering a change of flag.

Capital: Ljubljana
Area (sq. km): 20,300
Population: 2,000,000
Languages: Slovene
Currency: Tolar

Spain

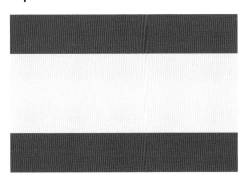

Kingdom of Spain

Spain was united in the 15th century and
soon after became a sea power capable
of building an empire, mainly in South
America. The red and yellow flag was
introduced on May 28, 1785, for use at
sea. The colors were taken from the
arms of Castile and Aragon. Spain is
confronted with several regions, such
as Catalonia and the Basque countries,
which seek more autonomy and fly
their own flags.

Capital: Madrid
Area (sq. km): 506,000
Population: 40,100,000
Languages: Spanish, Catalan, Basque
Currency: Euro

Sweden

Kingdom of Sweden

As Sweden was under Danish influence for
a long time, Sweden's flag is based on
the Danish Dannebrog flag. It was first
decreed as a battle standard at sea in
1569. The colors were taken from the
national coat of arms. Swedish Flag Day
became Sweden's National Day in 1983,
and is celebrated every June 6. This
was the date in 1523 on which the
foundations of Sweden, as a separate
state, were laid.

Capital: Stockholm
Area (sq. km): 450,000
Population: 8,900,000
Languages: Swedish
Currency: Swedish Krona

Switzerland

Swiss Confederation

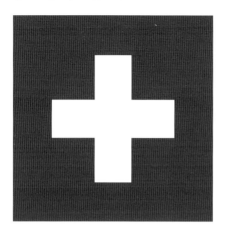

When used on land the Swiss flag is square, but when used in ships and yachts it is rectangular. Switzerland is named after Schwyz, the eldest of the 25 cantons. Schwyz uses a red banner with a white cross in the flag's canton. The Swiss flag, adopted December 12, 1889, is based on it. In turn, the Swiss banner shaped the flag of the Red Cross Society, which was founded by the Swiss Henri Dunant.

Capital: Bern
Area (sq. km): 41,300
Population: 7,200,000
Languages: German, French, Italian, Rheto-Roman
Currency: Swiss Franc

Transdnestria

Moldovian Dnestr Republic

Transdnestria declared independence from Moldova on September 2, 1991. This formerly Ukrainian region on the east bank of the Dnestr River was ceded to Moldova during the Soviet era. Ukrainians and Russians were anxious that Moldova would reunite with Romania after it ceded from the Soviet Union. The Transdnestrian flag, last confirmed on July 25, 2000, is the same as the Moldovian flag during the Soviet era.

Capital: Tiraspol
Area (sq. km): 4,000
Population: 600,000
Languages: Ukrainian, Russian
Currency: Transdnestrian Rouble

Turkey

Republic of Turkey

The Turkish flag, as it is today, first appeared in 1793, although the use of star and crescent goes back much earlier. Turkey is the small remainder of the vast Ottoman Empire, which broke into pieces after World War II. The country became a republic on October 29, 1923. Its flag was confirmed on June 5, 1936. Red is the traditional color of the Ottoman dynasty. The star and crescent are copied by other Islamic countries.

Capital: Ankara
Area (sq. km): 814,600
Population: 66,900,000
Languages: Turkish
Currency: Turkish Lira

Ukraine

Ukraine declared its independence from the Soviet Union on August 24, 1991. It was already briefly independent between 1918 and 1922, when it flew a light blue and yellow flag, which was re-established on September 4, 1991. Ukraine is known as the grain warehouse of the region, which is symbolized by the order of the colors. The light blue is the cloudless sky, needed to grow the corn, which is yellow at harvest.

Capital: Kiev
Area (sq. km): 603,700
Population: 50,200,000
Languages: Ukrainian, Russian
Currency: Hryvna

United Kingdom

United Kingdom of Great Britain and Northern Ireland

The Union Jack or Union Flag consists of the combined flags of England, Scotland, and Ireland. In its current form it was adopted on January 1, 1801, when Ireland joined the Union and the flag then received its red diagonal cross. The first Union Flag created in 1606 became the flag of the newly formed United Kingdom in 1707.

Capital: London
Area (sq. km): 241,750
Population: 58,700,000
Languages: English, Welsh, Gaelic
Currency: Pound Sterling

England

For a long time a red cross on a white field was the emblem of English soldiers and ships. It is the symbol of St. George, since 1277 England's patron saint. According to legend St. George courageously saved a princess by slaying a dragon. From 1606 until 1801, St. George's flag was used in English ships. Nowadays the flag, which is not official, is becoming a popular emblem among people who are proud to be English.

Capital: London
Area (sq. km): 130,400
Population: 49,000,000
Languages: English
Currency: Pound Sterling

Scotland

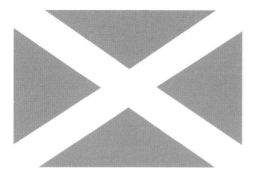

Legend has it that Scotland's St. Andrew's Cross was first seen near the village of Athelstaneford in AD 832. A Scottish King asked God for help in a battle and was rewarded by an x-shaped cloud formation in a blue sky. It was the shape of the cross on which St. Andrew, Scotland's patron saint, had been martyred. St. Andrew's Cross has always been popular among Scots proud to be independent.

Capital: Edinburgh
Area (sq. km): 77,100
Population: 5,200,000
Languages: English, Gaelic
Currency: Pound Sterling

Wales

Wales was already annexed by England when the Kingdom was formed in 1707. For this reason Wales is not represented in the Union Flag. Its flag— called "Y Draig Goch" (The Red Dragon) —was introduced at the beginning of the 20th century and received royal approval on February 23, 1959. Green and white are the traditional colors of Wales. The red dragon was adopted as a national symbol by the Welsh in the Middle Ages.

Capital: Cardiff
Area (sq. km): 20,750
Population: 2,900,000
Languages: Welsh, English
Currency: Pound Sterling

Northern Ireland

Northern Ireland, or Ulster, remained British when the island was partitioned in 1921. The official flag is the British Union Flag. However, Catholics fly the Irish flag to express their wish to unite with the Irish Republic. Protestants fly the Ulster flag, which was the official Northern Ireland flag between 1953 and 1972. This flag continues to be used to represent Northern Ireland at ceremonial and sporting occasions.

Capital: Belfast
Area (sq. km): 13,500
Population: 1,600,000
Languages: English
Currency: Pound Sterling

Alderney

King Edward VII approved the flag of the Channel Island of Alderney in December 1906. It shows St. George's Cross charged with a green disc with a yellow ornamental border and a lion walking upright holding a sprig of laurel in its left paw. It is not known how St. George's Cross, as well as the walking lion, became emblems of the island. Alderney is linked with Guernsey and is not part of the United Kingdom.

Capital: St. Anne
Area (sq. km): 8
Population: 2,200
Languages: English
Currency: Guernsey Pound

Guernsey

Bailiwick of Guernsey

The flag of the Channel Island of Guernsey was, for a long time, the same as that of England. The States (the local parliament), changed it to its current form on March 13, 1985. It combines St. George's Cross and the cross of William the Conqueror, as seen on the Bayeaux Tapestry. William's cross recalls the era Guernsey was part of the Duchy of Normandy. Guernsey is not part of the UK, but is owned by the Queen.

Capital: St. Peter Port
Area (sq. km): 65
Population: 60,000
Languages: English
Currency: Guernsey Pound

Jersey

Bailiwick of Jersey

For a long period of time, the Channel Island of Jersey used a white flag with a red St. Andrew's cross. The States (parliament) of Jersey decided on June 12, 1979, that the flag should be charged with the historical arms of the island. King Edward I of England granted these in 1290 to the Bailiff of Jersey. The crown on the shield recalls the House of Plantagenet. Jersey is a Crown Dependency.

Capital: St. Helier
Area (sq. km): 116
Population: 89,000
Languages: English
Currency: Jersey Pound

Isle of Man

The Isle of Man, set in the Irish Sea between England and Ireland, has been a dependency of the British Crown since June 21, 1765. Its red flag with a three-legged device, or "triskele," became the island's flag on January 1, 1933. It is not known why the three legs were adopted as royal arms of the old Manx kingdom in the 13th century. It is believed the Vikings brought the Manx Legs to the island. It might be an ancient sun emblem.

Capital: Douglas
Area (sq. km): 570
Population: 75,000
Languages: English, Manx
Currency: Isle of Man Pound

Shetland Islands

The Shetlands, a group of 100 islands, is part of Scotland and is neither independent nor autonomous. Students, who sought autonomy for the islands, first displayed the flag in 1969. In the flag, which is very popular in the islands, they expressed that the Shetlands had originally been part of Norway but are now Scottish. This is seen in the use of a Nordic cross and the Scottish colors blue and white.

Capital: Lerwick
Area (sq. km): 1,450
Population: 23,000
Languages: English
Currency: Pound sterling

Vatican City

State of the Vatican City

Vatican City, ruled by the Pope, is the world's smallest state. It was granted independence on June 7, 1929, when the flag was first displayed. Yellow and white were adopted as papal colors in 1808; the white field is charged with the emblem of Vatican City. This features the crossed keys of St. Peter supported by the papal crown. The keys give access to heaven and are kept by St. Peter, the first Pope.

Capital: Vatican City
Area (sq. km): 0.44
Population: 1,000
Languages: Italian, Latin
Currency: Euro

Yugoslavia

Federal Republic of Yugoslavia

In order to show it had abandoned communism, Yugoslavia dropped the central star from its flag on April 27, 1992. Yugoslavia was united in 1919, when the flag, in the pan-Slav colors, was first displayed. The country collapsed into five countries in 1991–1992. Serbia, Montenegro, and Kosovo are officially still part of Yugoslavia, but it is unlikely that the country will exist for long.

Capital: Belgrade
Area (sq. km): 102,200
Population: 10,700,000
Languages: Serbian, Albanian, Hungarian
Currency: New Dinar

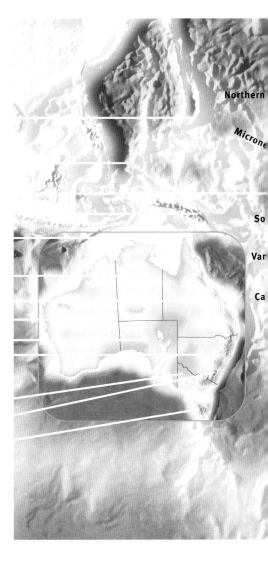

Guam

Palau

Nauru

Papua New Guinea

Torres Strait

Northern Territory

Queensland

Western Australia

South Australia
New South Wales

Victoria

Australian Capital Territory

Tasmania

Northern

Microne

So

Var

Ca

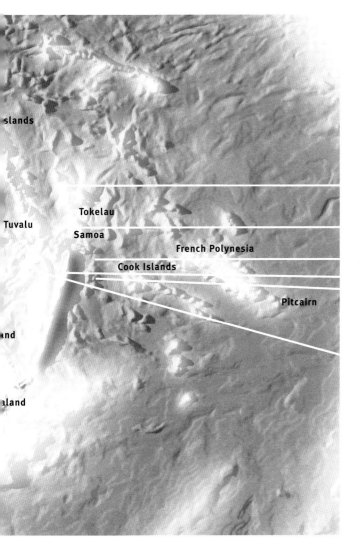

slands

Kiribati

Tokelau

Tuvalu

Wallis and
Futuna

Samoa

French Polynesia

American Samoa

Cook Islands

Tonga

Niue

Pitcairn

ınd

Fiji

ıland

OCEANIA covers nearly half of the world, but at the same time it is the smallest continent. Oceania is a vast ocean, studded by thousands of islands. The largest are Australia and New Zealand; the majority are tiny and often form archipelagos with neighboring islands. A number are still ruled as overseas territories by Washington, London, or Paris and this is reflected in the flags flown.

British and Dutch ships brought the first flags to Oceania. The captains of these vessels planted flags on the shores of Australia and New Zealand to claim them for their country. Eventually they became British colonies and for a long period of time, they only flew the Union Flag.

Before Australia was established as a federation in 1901, it consisted of six British colonies. They set about designing their own flags in the second half of the 19th century. The Colonial Defence Act of 1865 empowered all Australian colonies to provide, maintain, and use vessels of war. These ships were allowed to fly the British blue ensign, with the colonial seal or badge in the fly. This Act may be seen as the starting point of modern flag design in the Pacific region.

Europeans began to take an interest in the tiny islands scattered across the Pacific Ocean in the first half of the 19th century. The British, French, and Germans were eager to conclude treaties with the local rulers to protect them against enemies. In these treaties, it was ruled that local ships must fly their own distinctive flags. As there were none, the local kings designed them from scratch. European interest and influence in this region is probably best seen in the flag of the Kingdom of Tonga. In 1830, its king converted to

Christianity. When the country needed a flag in 1864, the king's First Minister, the European Rev. S. Baker designed it. It shows a red field, signifying the sacrifice of Christ's blood, and a white canton charged with a red cross, to represent Christianity.

In the second half of the 19th century, the protectorates were successively annexed by the powers, which had promised to protect these states. The United Kingdom, France, and Germany managed to control half the world, a situation which changed at the end of World War I. Germany had to cede all its overseas territories. Its islands in the Pacific were

Natives of Yap Island, Micronesia, carry a variety of flags in celebration of United Nations Day.

governed by Japan for the League of Nations as a Trust Territory. Australia was appointed to administer Samoa and Nauru as UN Trust Territories. As it was among the nations who had lost World War II, Japan had to cede its Pacific islands to the United Nations, the successor of the League of Nations. The United States was appointed by the United Nations to administer these former German islands as Trust Territories.

Australia and New Zealand became completely independent within the British Commonwealth by the 1931 Statute of Westminster. This was achieved because they were mainly inhabited and ruled by people of European origin. By keeping their colonial-styled flags, these new countries showed that they had not renounced their links with Britain.

Apart from the British dependencies in the Pacific, none of the archipelagos used distinguishing flags. The UN Trust Territory of Western Samoa was the first, in 1948, to establish its own flag, an example followed by other groups of islands.

After World War II, the call for emancipation of all other Pacific islands became louder, triggered by was happening in Africa and Central America. Western Samoa was the first non-Western Pacific country to achieve independence in 1962, after a period of autonomy. Other countries gradually followed Samoa's example.

Blue plays an important role in the flag of the Pacific island states. In most cases it symbolizes the Pacific Ocean, or the United Nations, which has played an important role in their recent political history. The British influence in the Pacific region is still visible in the flags of the new nations, such as Tuvalu and Niue.

New Zealand and Australia also have a miniature version of the Union Flag in their national flags. Both countries, however, have growing numbers of people who would like to see their flags cleared of the emblems of their colonial heritage. Australia has already held several competitions for a new flag design. Kangaroos and Southern Crosses are favorite emblems.

American Samoa

Territory of American Samoa

The American Samoan flag was first displayed on April 27, 1960, the date on which 60 years earlier the United States of America took possession of the islands. The colors are taken from the Stars and Stripes. The American eagle holds in its talons traditional Samoan chief's attributes: the fue, or fly switch, (seen as a symbol of wisdom) and the nifo oti, a traditional Samoan knife and war symbol.

Capital: Pago Pago
Area (sq. km): 200
Population: 65,000
Languages: English, Samoan
Currency: US Dollar

Australia

Commonwealth of Australia

Six British colonies agreed to unite as Australia on January 1, 1901. When the newspaper *The Review of Reviews* organized a flag design competition, over 30,000 designs were submitted. The £200 prize was divided among five people. The flag became official in February 1903. The constellation shown is the Southern Cross, the large star under the Union Flag represents the Australian federation.

Capital: Canberra
Area (sq. km): 7,741,200
Population: 19,300,000
Languages: English
Currency: Australian Dollar

Australian Capital Territory

The flag of the Australian Capital Territory (ACT) of Canberra was adopted on March 25, 1993. Interested citizens provided flag designs in open competitions held in 1988 and 1992. Each time, however, there was no agreement on a particular design. The flag adopted was the outcome of community consultation, which showed that citizens liked the Southern Cross and a modified form of the Canberra City coat of Arms.

Capital: Canberra
Area (sq. km): 2,360
Population: 315,000

New South Wales

The earliest badge of New South Wales was the red cross of St. George, authorized in an Order-in-Council in 1869. The badge took its current form on February 15, 1876. The cross was enriched with an English lion and four eight-pointed yellow stars. The lion symbolized the links with England and the four stars represented the Southern Cross.

Capital: Sydney
Area (sq. km): 801,600
Population: 6,600,000

Northern Territory

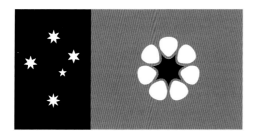

The flag of the Northern Territory was first flown on July 1, 1978, to celebrate the granting of self-government to the territory. The Northern Territory broke with the Australian tradition of adopting flags based on the Union Flag by choosing the design of artist Robert Ingpen. Black, white, and ochre are the official colors of the territory. The flower in the fly is a stylized Sturt's Desert Rose, the territory's floral emblem.

Capital: Darwin
Area (sq. km): 1,350,000
Population: 200,000

Queensland

Queensland was created when it separated from New South Wales on December 10, 1859. Its first flag showing the head of Queen Victoria proved too difficult to produce. The current flag came into use on November 29, 1876. The British blue ensign-styled flag is charged with a Maltese Cross and a crown. No one knows why this cross was used, but it might be a stylized version of the Southern Cross constellation.

Capital: Brisbane
Area (sq. km): 1,730,000
Population: 3,600,000

South Australia

The State Flag of South Australia was authorized on January 13, 1904. It is a blue ensign charged with the state badge. The badge depicts the piping shrike with open wings standing on a branch of a gum tree. The piping shrike, or white backed magpie, is found in open timbered country in the eastern part of South Australia. The badge was originally drawn by Robert Craig of the School of Arts.

Capital: Adelaide
Area (sq. km): 983,000
Population: 1,500,000

Tasmania

Like all six original states of Australia, Tasmania has a colonial-styled British blue ensign charged with the coat of arms in the fly. It was first adopted on November 29, 1875. The arms show a lion, but it is not known why. It is possible that it was meant to indicate links with England. The same lion appears in the Tasmanian coat of arms. This flag was officially approved as the State flag of Tasmania on December 3, 1975.

Capital: Hobart
Area (sq. km): 68,400
Population: 471,000

Victoria

The flag of Victoria was adopted on November 30, 1877, when the crown was added to the constellation of the Southern Cross, in the fly. The crown symbolized Victoria's ties with Queen Victoria and Britain. The original design was first flown in the HMVS *Nelson*, Victoria's first colonial warship, on February 9, 1870. It is very likely that the Australian flag is modeled on Victoria's state flag.

Capital: Melbourne
Area (sq. km): 227,500
Population: 4,800,000

Western Australia

Western Australia was first known as the Swan River Settlement. The black swan has been associated with Western Australia from earliest times. An Aboriginal legend states that the Bilbulman tribe were originally black swans, but changed into men. The swan was introduced on a yellow badge of Western Australia on November 27, 1875. The direction it swam was changed toward the inside of the flag in 1953.

Capital: Perth
Area (sq. km): 2,530,000
Population: 1,900,000

Aboriginals

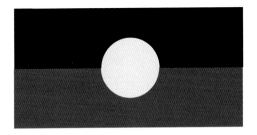

The Aboriginal Flag was designed by Aboriginal artist Harold Thomas and was first raised in Adelaide on National Aboriginal Day. The flag was legalized as an Australian flag on July 14, 1995. The black stripe represents the Aboriginal people and the red stands for both the earth and the spiritual relationship the Aboriginals have with the land. The yellow disc symbolizes the sun, which is the source of all life.

Torres Strait Islander

The Torres Strait Islander flag, designed by Bernard Namok of Thursday Island, was legalized as an official Australian flag on July 14, 1995. Torres Strait Islanders are an indigenous people having limited autonomy. The green stripes represent the land, the black stripes the Torres Strait Islander, and the blue field represents the sea. In the flag's center is a white dhari, a traditional headdress, and a star representing unity.

Norfolk Island

Territory of Norfolk Island

Norfolk Island was discovered in 1774 by Captain Cook and gained autonomy from Australia in 1979. The nine member Legislative Assembly approved the flag on January 11, 1980. The tree in the central white stripe, which is a little broader than the two green stripes, is a silhouette of a Norfolk Island pine. This tree is characteristic of the island. The abundant vegetation of the island is symbolized by the green panels.

Capital: Kingston
Area (sq. km): 35
Population: 2,100
Languages: English
Currency: Australian Dollar

Cook Islands

The Cook Islands are a dependency of New Zealand. The flag dates from June 22, 1979, when it was approved by the local parliament. Although the islands are a New Zealand dependency they use a British blue ensign. For the Cook Islands, this reflects their links with New Zealand. The fifteen white stars represent the main islands of the archipelago. They are set in a circle to express they are equal.

Capital: Avarua
Area (sq. km): 240
Population: 21,000
Languages: English, Maori
Currency: New Zealand Dollar

Fiji

Republic of the Fiji Islands

Although Fiji became independent from the United Kingdom on October 10, 1970, it retained a British-styled flag. The design was selected by a competition won jointly by Mr. Robi Wilcock and Mrs. Murray MacKenzie of Suva. The blue field represents the Pacific Ocean. The shield in the flag's fly depicts an English lion and cross to recall the links with that country, and some local agricultural products, such as bananas and coconuts.

Capital: Suva
Area (sq. km): 18,330
Population: 796,000
Languages: English, Fijian, Hindi
Currency: Fiji Dollar

French Polynesia

Territory of French Polynesia

Since September 6, 1984, Polynesia has had internal autonomy within the French entity. The island adopted a special flag the following November 23 to indicate its newly gained status. It was based on the flag used by independent Tahiti before 1880, when it became French. The new flag was charged with an image of a Polynesian piroguc. It had always played an important role in the daily life of the Polynesians.

Capital: Papeete
Area (sq. km): 4,200
Population: 258,000
Languages: French, Tahitian
Currency: CFP Franc

Guam

Territory of Guam

The Guam flag was designed in 1917 by Mrs. Helen Paul, wife of the US Navy Public Works Officer. Guam, the largest of the Mariana Islands, has been an American territory since 1899. The blue field represents the Pacific Ocean and the skies over the island. In the center is the island's seal in the shape of a traditional Chamorro sling stone used as a weapon. The red border represents the blood shed by the Chamorro people.

Capital: Hagotna
Area (sq. km): 550
Population: 160,000
Languages: English
Currency: US Dollar

Kiribati

Republic of Kiribati

Kiribati (pronounced as Kiribas) consists of 36 atolls covering a vast part of the Pacific Ocean. The flag was first hoisted on independence from Britain on July 12, 1979, and shows the image of the national arms. The frigate bird represents power and freedom. The tropical sun shows that Kiribati lies astride the equator. The blue and white waves symbolize the Pacific Ocean, which surround every island.

Capital: Tarawa
Area (sq. km): 725
Population: 90,000
Languages: English
Currency: Australian Dollar

Marshall Islands

Republic of the Marshall Islands

The Marshall Islands were administered as a UN Trust Territory by the USA until December 1990 when they were granted independence. They received autonomy on May 1, 1979, and at this time the flag was first displayed. Blue stands for the Pacific. The 24 points of the star symbolize the 24 municipalities of the country; the four larger points represent the four larger atolls. Orange represents bravery, white is for hope.

Capital: Majuro
Area (sq. km): 180
Population: 650,000
Languages: English, Marshallese
Currency: US Dollar

Micronesia

Federated States of Micronesia

The Micronesian flag was adopted on November 30, 1978, when the four groups of islands were administered as a UN Trust Territory by the USA. The blue is similar to the blue in the UN flag. This is to recall the role it played in the history of the islands. The four stars represent the four groups of islands—Chuuk, Kosrae, Pohnpei, and Yap—which fly flags of their own.

Capital: Palikir
Area (sq. km): 700
Population: 121,000
Languages: English, eight local languages
Currency: US Dollar

Nauru

Republic of Nauru

The flag of Nauru should be read as a map. The island was granted independence by New Zealand on January 31, 1968, when the flag was first hoisted. The blue field symbolizes the Pacific Ocean. The yellow stripe is the equator, which runs just north of Nauru. The midline represents the International Dateline and the star represents Nauru. Each of its 12 points represents an original Nauruan tribe.

Capital: Yaren
Area (sq. km): 20
Population: 11,500
Languages: English, Nauruan
Currency: Australian Dollar

New Caledonia

Territory of New Caledonia and Dependencies

New Caledonia is a French dependent territory since 1854 and served as a convict settlement from 1871 to 1896. New Caledonia has no flag. The indigenous Kanak people support independence, but the French majority do not. The Kanak people fly a pro-independence flag, while the French show the Tricolore. A referendum on independence is planned before 2018.

Capital: Noumea
Area (sq. km): 19,100
Population: 208,000
Languages: French, 33 Melanesian-Polynesian dialects
Currency: CFP Franc

New Zealand

New Zealand was a British colony when the current flag was adopted on June 12, 1902. It was not changed when the country achieved Dominion status on September 9, 1907. The New Zealand flag has the form of a British blue ensign, which shows that the country still has close links with Britain. The four stars represent the constellation of the Southern Cross in a stylized form. (In reality, the constellation consists of five stars.)

Capital: Wellington
Area (sq. km): 270,500
Population: 3,950,000
Languages: English, Maori
Currency: New Zealand Dollar

Niue

Republic of Niue

Niue is a New Zealand dependency that adopted its current flag on October 15, 1975. The yellow field represents the bright sunshine and the warm feeling of the Niuean people. The Union Flag recalls that the British proclaimed the island a protectorate in 1900. The large star on the blue disc in the Union Flag symbolizes the self-governing status of Niue, standing alone in the Pacific. The small stars refer to New Zealand.

Capital: Alofi
Area (sq. km): 260
Population: 2,100
Languages: English, Niuean
Currency: New Zealand Dollar

Northern Marianas

Commonwealth of the Northern Mariana Islands

The USA administered the Northern Marianas after World War II as a UN Trust Territory until 1986. It is now a self-governing US territory. The basic design of the flag was adopted on March 31, 1972. It showed a blue field, representing the Pacific, with an ancient latte stone to represent the Chamorro culture. The star represents unity. Since 1985, the flag has been charged with a mwaar, a flower chain, to represent Carolinian culture.

Capital: Garapan
Area (sq. km): 450
Population: 66,000
Languages: English
Currency: US Dollar

Palau

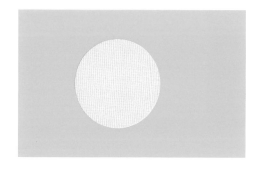

Republic of Palau

Palau became fully independent on October 1, 1994. The flag was first hoisted on January 1, 1981, when Palau became an autonomous republic, but was administered as a UN Trust Territory by the USA. The blue field, which is similar to the UN flag blue, recalls the role the UN played in the recent history of Palau and symbolizes the Pacific. The yellow disk is a full moon, which represents peace, love, and tranquility.

Capital: Koror
Area (sq. km): 460
Population: 19,000
Languages: English, Palauan
Currency: US Dollar

Papua New Guinea

Independent State of Papua New Guinea

Susan Karike Hahome was 18 when she designed her country's flag. It was first displayed on July 1, 1971, and was retained as the national flag when Papua New Guinea became independent on September 16, 1975. Red and black are predominant colors in the country's native art. The constellation refers to Australia, which administered the country as a UN Trusteeship. The bird of paradise is peculiar to the country.

Capital: Port Moresby
Area (sq. km): 462,800
Population: 4,950,000
Languages: English, Hiri Motu
Currency: Kina

Pitcairn

Pitcairn Islands

Queen Elizabeth II approved Pitcairn's flag on April 2, 1984. It is a traditional blue ensign, revealing that the territory is a British dependency. The island was first settled in 1790 by the mutineers from the Bounty; this is symbolized in the coat of arms in the flag's fly. It depicts the Bible and the anchor of the ship the Bounty. The triangle symbolizes the island's cliffs and the blue represents the Pacific Ocean.

Capital: Adamstown
Area (sq. km): 5
Population: 50
Languages: English
Currency: New Zealand Dollar

Samoa

Independent State of Samoa

Samoa adopted its current flag on February 11, 1949, when the islands where administered by New Zealand as a UN Trust Territory. The flag was retained as the national flag when independence was achieved on January 1, 1962. The five stars represent the Southern Cross. The red field symbolizes courage, white stands for purity, and blue for freedom. Samoa's national anthem is named "The Banner of Freedom."

Capital: Apia
Area (sq. km): 2,800
Population: 179,000
Languages: English, Samoan
Currency: Tala

Solomon Islands

Queen Elizabeth granted the national flag of the Solomon Islands by Royal Warrant on November 18, 1977, anticipating independence from Britain. This was achieved on July 7, 1978. The upper blue triangle represents the Pacific Ocean and the blue sky. The lower green triangle stands for the islands, which are covered with forests. The five stars represent the five groups of islands. The yellow stripe stands for the sun.

Capital: Honiara
Area (sq. km): 28,900
Population: 470,000
Languages: English, 80 local languages
Currency: Solomon Islands Dollar

Tokelau

Tokelau, or Union Islands, has been a territory of New Zealand since 1949. For this reason, the New Zealand flag is also the national flag of Tokelau. A competition for a flag design has been postponed several times. Sometimes a local blue flag, with three stars to represent the three atolls and a silhouette of a local palm tree, is flown. Most of the Tokelauan people live in New Zealand.

Capital: Fakaofo
Area (sq. km): 12
Population: 1,500
Languages: English, Tokelauan
Currency: New Zealand Dollar

Tonga

Kingdom of Tonga

The constitution of Tonga reads: "The Flag of Tonga shall never be altered but shall always be the flag of the Kingdom." The flag dates from 1862 when King George Tupoi I decreed a flag to symbolize his Christian faith. (He was a convert.) The colors red and white stand for liberty and peace through the Christian religion. Red is Jesus' blood, shed on the cross. Between 1900 and June 4, 1970, Tonga was British.

Capital: Nuku'alofa
Area (sq. km): 750
Population: 103,500
Languages: English, Tongan
Currency: Pa'anga

Tuvalu

Tuvalu achieved independence from Britain on October 1, 1978, when the current flag was first hoisted. The Union Flag in the canton expresses the islands' links with the United Kingdom. The blue field represents the Pacific Ocean and the nine stars in the fly stand for the nine islands. Anti-commonwealth feelings led to a new flag for Tuvalu in 1995, without any representation of the Union Flag. The original design was readopted on April 10, 1997.

Capital: Fongafale
Area (sq. km): 25
Population: 11,000
Languages: English, Tuvaluan
Currency: Australian Dollar

Vanuatu

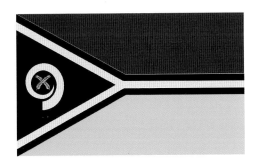

Republic of Vanuatu

Vanuatu achieved independence from Britain and France on July 30, 1980, but its flag had already been adopted on March 5. Black symbolizes the Melanesian people. Green is the island's vegetation, and red is symbolic of blood. The Y-shape depicts the geographical outline of the archipelago. The boar's tusk is a traditional symbol of prosperity, while the ferns symbolize peace, with their 39 fronds representing the members of parliament.

Capital: Port-Vila
Area (sq. km): 12,200
Population: 196,000
Languages: English, French, Pidgin
Currency: Vatu

Wallis and Futuna

Territory of Wallis and Futuna Islands

Wallis and Futuna is a French territory and therefore flies the French Tricolore as the national flag. The islands were independent kingdoms until France annexed them on November 19, 1886. The kings added the French flag onto their own flag. These flags are sometimes used nowadays as signs of autonomy, but do not have a legal status.

Capital: Mata-Utu
Area (sq. km): 275
Population: 16,000
Languages: French, Wallisian
Currency: CFP Franc

List of Flags